Connecting

Content and Academic Language

for English Learners and Struggling Students
Grades 2–6

Connecting

Content and Academic Language

for English Learners and Struggling Students Grades 2–6

Ruth Swinney
Patricia Velasco

Foreword by **Ofelia García**

CORWIN
A SAGE Company

CORWIN
A SAGE Company

For information:

Corwin
A SAGE Company
2455 Teller Road
Thousand Oaks, California 91320
www.corwin.com

SAGE Ltd.
1 Oliver's Yard
55 City Road
London, EC1Y 1SP
United Kingdom

SAGE Pvt. Ltd.
B 1/I 1 Mohan Cooperative Industrial Area
Mathura Road, New Delhi 110 044
India

SAGE Asia-Pacific Pte. Ltd.
33 Pekin Street #02–01
Far East Square
Singapore 048763

Acquisitions Editor: Carol Chambers Collins
Associate Editor: Megan Bedell
Editorial Assistant: Sarah Bartlett
Production Editor: Veronica Stapleton
Copy Editor: Matthew Adams
Typesetter: C&M Digitals (P) Ltd.
Proofreader: Dennis W. Webb
Indexer: Sheila Bodell
Cover Designer: Karine Hovsepian
Permissions Editor: Adele Hutchinson

Copyright © 2011 by Corwin

All rights reserved. When forms and sample documents are included, their use is authorized only by educators, local school sites, and/or noncommercial or nonprofit entities that have purchased the book. Except for that usage, no part of this book may be reproduced or utilized in any form or by any means, electronic or mechanical, including photocopying, recording, or by any information storage and retrieval system, without permission in writing from the publisher.

All trade names and trademarks recited, referenced, or reflected herein are the property of their respective owners who retain all rights thereto.

Printed in the United States of America

Library of Congress Cataloging-in-Publication Data

Swinney, Ruth.

Connecting content and academic language for English learners and struggling students, grades 2–6 / Ruth Swinney, Patricia Velasco; foreword by Ofelia Garcia.

p. cm.
Includes bibliographical references and index.

ISBN 978-1-4129-8843-8 (pbk.)

1. Content area reading. 2. Language arts (Elementary) 3. Reading—Remedial teaching. 4. English language—Study and teaching (Elementary)—Foreign speakers. I. Velasco, Patricia, 1973- II. Garcia, Ofelia. III. Title.

LB1050.455.S95 2011
372.6—dc22
2011006847

This book is printed on acid-free paper.

11 12 13 14 15 10 9 8 7 6 5 4 3 2 1

Contents

Additional materials related to *Connecting Content and Academic Language for English Learners and Struggling Students, Grades 2–6,* can be found at http://www.corwin.com/connectingcontent4ell

List of Illustrations

CHAPTER 1

CHAPTER 2

CHAPTER 6

CHAPTER 7

Foreword

Finding Cats and Dogs in the Zoo

Ofelia García

The first vignette in Swinney and Velasco's masterful *Integrating Content and Language Goals for English Learners and Struggling Students, Grades 2–6*, introduces us to a second grader who is learning English. When the teacher asks the class what animals they want to see in the zoo, the girl uses the words she knows in English to reply: "Cats and dogs." The teacher ignores her response and moves on to other children. Swinney and Velasco point out that the teacher's dismissal of this girl's class participation misses an important point. The child herself, upon returning from the zoo, is able to correctly articulate that there were no cats and dogs. Indeed, there would have been a way for the teacher to find the girl's "cats and dogs" in initially talking about the zoo. This is precisely what Swinney and Velasco guide teachers to do through this book.

The question of how to teach students who are learning English, those who may be more aptly called "emergent bilinguals" (García & Kleifgen, 2010), has become a minefield, with scholars arguing for more or less use of students' home languages in the classroom, and with bilingual education under attack. Swinney and Velasco avoid the minefields by focusing on only one thing—the teacher's expertise in developing the academic language of emergent bilinguals, whether in bilingual, ESL, or mainstream classrooms. In fact, all of the examples come from different classroom contexts. The focus is then on the careful and intentional planning to use and practice academic language. To find the cats and dogs in the conversation about the zoo, the teacher has to be vigilant and to change her lenses so as to develop a new vision of possibilities.

Swinney and Velasco's book precisely offers a new close-up vision of how to teach emergent bilinguals. Whereas most texts focus on macro-organizational classroom features that sometimes blur the vision, Swinney and Velasco's approach is telescopic, bringing into focus the micro-elements that teachers of emergent bilingual students must manage. The book carefully and intentionally scaffolds for teachers what they must plan and do in order to develop not only new planning and teaching strategies, but also a new close-up vision.

In the many years that I have worked in this field, I have not found another book that offers such minute and careful details focused on the development of academic language for emergent bilinguals. The issue of which language to use, whether English or the home language, doesn't enter the picture. It is taken for granted that the context will determine the language use—whether English or the child's home language. What is important in language use is not the language per se, but the *type* of language that children use. Thus, over and over again, the authors repeat that academic language has to be planned. And yet, the authors make it clear that the starting point of academic language development lies elsewhere. Teaching and learning emergent bilinguals start with the children's background knowledge, their own cats and dogs, and with social language and conversation.

The academic language of emergent bilinguals, the book tells us, is developed through three building blocks: (a) background knowledge, (b) a curriculum of talk that includes critical thinking skills, and (c) the components of read alouds and shared reading and writing. It is precisely these three building blocks that are weaved throughout the book. In the first part, they constitute the first three chapters, with each building block developed in detail. In the second part of the book, each of the three building blocks is manifested in disciplinary and interdisciplinary learning units (language arts, social studies, science, interdisciplinary unit) enacted by teachers of different age groups and in bilingual or ESL classrooms. It is as if the telescope that Swinney and Velasco offer teachers is collapsible, not only offering a different vision, but also enabled by an instrument whose shape is consistent and whose parts neatly fit into each other. Thus, although the vision is up-close, it is also integrated, whole, and expansive.

What makes this book unlike any other is the careful build-up of exact strategies. The authors anchor their examples not only in real classrooms with real teachers and children, but also in authentic instructional strategies. For example, the chapters in Part II all offer a template for planning the unit, but in addition, the authors include and describe exact tools to be used. Each of the chapters in this part has a section called "Breaking the Plan Into Doable Parts," and specific tools are identified and modeled for each of the components. Graphic organizers, conception definition maps, partnership strategies, semantic webbing, word walls, and photo analysis work sheets are all part of the toolboxes provided. This is especially evident in Part I of the book. In Chapter 1, specific strategies for teaching vocabulary, as well as syntax and morphology, are carefully detailed. In Chapter 2, examples of strategies to develop listening, as well as oral abilities, are carefully described. And Chapter 3 provides not only detailed examples of structures of balanced literacy, but even the exact words that teachers need to use before, during, and after read alouds and shared reading and writing. The result is that more than a map or guide is offered in this book. Instead, minute details that would be helpful for any teacher, but especially for those teaching children who need to develop academic language, are presented throughout the book.

At a time in which the nation's children are increasingly bilingual, this book offers the support that all teachers need to develop the academic language of emergent bilinguals. Swinney and Velasco make the very important point that the curriculum for these students needs to be the same challenging one as that offered other students. The book instead focuses on amplifying the teaching strategies and modifying the instructional strategies so as to recognize the emergent bilinguals' "cats and dogs," and then build upon them. Swinney and Velasco offer teachers of emergent bilinguals ways of seeing emergent bilingual children with new lenses and hearing their words with new tools. Only then, by listening closely to their conversations and their thinking, will teachers be able to adjust their vision of these children as most capable learners, and thus plan appropriately for the development of their academic language. Cats and dogs can indeed be found in conversations about the zoo in classrooms, and Swinney and Velasco give teachers ways of leading emergent bilinguals to also find the lions, and tigers, and bears that they're sure to find if they're allowed to walk on the same challenging curricular road as all the other children.

REFERENCE

García, O., & Kleifgen, J. (2010). *Educating emergent bilinguals. Policies, programs and practices for English language learners.* New York, NY: Teachers College Press.

Acknowledgments

W e want to thank many people who have been indispensable in writing this book: Pedro de la Cruz, the principal of PS 165, allowed us to work and observe teachers without any limitations; we are so thankful for his generosity. There are many teachers who worked with us in the past 2 years, too many to mention, without whose input we could not have written this book, but we are particularly in debt to Rachel Bard, Grace Stevenson, Karen Cruz, and Annely Ianello, from PS 165, for sharing their experience, their classrooms, and their concerns with us. The years spent working alongside Lucy Calkins and our colleagues at the Reading and Writing Project have enriched us in immeasurable ways and helped us to understand how balanced literacy can support the language growth of ELs and struggling students; we continue to draw on our rich experiences at the Project. We want to extend our gratitude to Herlinda Cancino and Jossie O'Neill, who generously gave us time and feedback. We thank them for their contributions to this book. Last, but certainly not least, to Ofelia García, who was our book's godmother, we are so thankful! And of course to our husbands Bob and Pablo, and our children, we could not have done it without your support!

PUBLISHER'S ACKNOWLEDGMENTS

Corwin gratefully acknowledges the contributions of the following reviewers:

Emme Barnes, Curriculum Facilitator
Charlotte Mecklenburg Schools
Charlotte, NC

Irma Guadarrama, Professor
University of Texas Pan American
Edinburg, TX

Cathy Hooper, Literacy Coordinator
Henderson Independent School District
Henderson, TX

Stephanie Malin, Response to Intervention/School Improvement Specialist
Beaverton School District
Beaverton, OR

Jossie O'Neill, Director of Partnerships & Outreach
The Gateway School of New York
The Gateway Middle School
New York, NY

Elizabeth Roberts Scaduto, K–12 Director of ESL
Riverhead Central School District
Riverhead, NY

Sue Summers, ELL Teacher
Boise School District
Boise, ID

Darlene Vigil, Assistant Principal
Albuquerque Public Schools
Albuquerque, NM

About the Authors

**Ruth Swinney** is a native of Colombia, S.A. She started her career as a bilingual teacher in New York City. In 1984 she founded one of the first dual language programs in New York City in PS 84, and subsequently became director of bilingual and dual language programs for a large district in NYC. In this role she supervised bilingual and ESL programs and developed seven model dual language programs for the District. When she became principal of PS 165 (Manhattan) she set up a nationally recognized dual language program at the same time that she turned around one of the bottom schools in the city. She has won numerous awards for her work with second language learners and for her achievements as a principal. After retiring, she worked with the Reading and Writing Project at Teachers College, Columbia University, heading the principal work, and the ELL department. Currently she works as a consultant.

**Patricia Velasco** started her career as a speech pathologist in Mexico City. After finishing her EdD in the United States, she established a Staff Development Institute (Casa de la Ciencia) that works with indigenous bilingual children and their teachers in San Cristobal de las Casas, Chiapas, Mexico. After she moved to New York City, she first worked for the Reading and Writing Project at Teachers College, Columbia University, as a staff developer supporting teachers all across New York City in addressing the literacy and language needs of English language learners. In addition, she was part of the faculty at Teachers College, Columbia University. Currently she is Assistant Professor of Education at Queens College, City University of New York, where she coordinates the Bilingual Program.

PART I

The Language Component

From Social to Academic Language

Introduction

Making Content Accessible to English Learners and Struggling Students

This book addresses the challenges that teachers of English learners and struggling students face as they try to meet the language needs of their students within the increasing demands of the curriculum. The academic language that is needed to succeed in school entails a broad knowledge of words, grammar, and pragmatic conventions for expression, understanding, and interpretation; it also requires frequent interaction with books and conversations about topics that are outside of everyday experiences. Many students struggle throughout their years in school because their background knowledge and language skills do not match school expectations: Words associated with content and academic knowledge fall outside their everyday interactions, and many children have never heard them; sentences can be long and complicated; summarizing, synthesizing, and retelling information is often an insurmountable obstacle that grows in importance as students move up in the grades. Some of these struggling students may be EL students who have entered school with interrupted schooling or with low literacy skills in their native language. Other students may have been born in the United States, but they also lack literacy skills in English.

We refer to English learners using the acronym EL. In some school systems, teachers and administrators refer to those students as ELL (English Language Learners) or LEP (Limited English Proficient) students.

We have written this book taking into consideration the challenges that teachers face on a daily basis, working with multilingual students and different levels of academic proficiency in their classrooms. Grouping children according to fixed stages of language acquisition sounds plausible, but it is not feasible within the time allotted for instruction and the demands of the curriculum, particularly when we are asking teachers to group students according to their academic proficiency. Some EL students may not have the language to work with an advanced group within the classroom, but they may have the academic proficiency in their native language to understand the content. Some students may be proficient in English but may lack the literacy skills to deal with advanced academic content. Throughout the units that we present in this book, we scaffold the work for recent EL arrivals, but we do not divide the students according to their level of English proficiency; instead, we focus on language development for every activity we plan.

The National Core Standards outline the skills and knowledge that every student (including EL students) should have in English language arts and mathematics. Teachers have the ultimate responsibility to ensure that all their students meet standards in order to succeed in school, but the major challenge they face in achieving this goal is making the content accessible to their struggling students. To move at the pace the curriculum demands, some teachers often resort to simplifying the material or cover it superficially. The main contribution that our book makes is to show teachers that they have other options rather than simplifying the material. They can scaffold the content that the unit requires, and at the same time they can focus on teaching the language that will enable the students to succeed. Throughout the book we offer ideas teachers can use to plan their units of study integrating content and language goals to meet the needs of their most challenging students.

The book is divided into two parts. The first section focuses on language components. It integrates ways of developing language that are often studied separately—conversation, vocabulary, morphology, and syntax. These elements are explained and incorporated into language goals in the sample units of study. We focus on the basic knowledge that teachers of ELs and struggling students should know about background knowledge and how it affects learning and language; they need this knowledge to support the linguistic and academic growth of their students. Within this section of the book, the continuum of social to academic language is examined. Researchers agree that the mastery of academic language plays a determinant role in school achievement (Baker, 2006; Cummins, 1979, 2000, 2007; Snow, Griffin, & Burns, 1998; Skutnabb-Kangas & Toukomaa, 1976). We stress the role that conversation plays in the development of academic language and present ways to develop language skills through a curriculum of talk.

The second section of the book focuses on lesson components. It shows teachers how they can use specific structures of balanced literacy—read aloud, shared reading, and shared writing—to develop background knowledge and to teach the language skills students need to understand the content. We provide specific units of study in language arts, social studies, and science, as well as a thematic unit. This section presents multiple strategies for teachers to structure and deepen the classroom conversations within each unit of study and templates to organize language goals. In this second section of the book, we have included theory to practice connections that link theoretical elements presented in the first section of the book to the units of study developed in the second section.

The basic premise of our book is that learning academic language has to be planned. Students have multiple opportunities to talk, discuss, and analyze the words and structures that are pertinent to the content being developed and multiple reading and writing experiences, both independently and within a group. This view of planning for academic language development entails that we are not viewing academic language as occurring in fixed, developmental stages, but rather that it requires exposure, practice, and teaching. For every sample unit, we provide planning templates to help guide teachers as they integrate content and language goals. These guides will help teachers scaffold the unit, breaking down essential components to make the language and content comprehensible to ELs. In addition we provide a self-assessment guide for the teacher at the end of each unit.

This book was written with teachers by our side and is for teachers in bilingual settings, in regular classrooms, and for ESL teachers. We hope that it can be valuable in teacher training programs where we have successfully taught teachers to incorporate language objectives into all their planning. Our ultimate goal is to empower our students to develop the language skills that will allow them to flourish in school. Note: An appendix containing the templates we use throughout the units is available online at http://www.corwin.com/connectingcontent4ell.

1

Building Language

How and Why

This chapter aims to

- Explore the importance of different aspects that impact *language development*
- Provide explicit *strategies* for triggering background knowledge using a variety of graphic organizers to structure new concepts
- Provide *activities* to help teachers enrich the vocabulary of their students
- Focus on *language structures* that are challenging for second language learners and provide *suggestions* on how to present them to EL and struggling students

Background knowledge is not only essential when we acquire new information but is important for vocabulary development (Marzano, 2004). Vocabulary plays an essential role in the process of understanding new concepts and storing them in our memory (Snow, Griffin, & Burns, 2005). Many ELs and struggling learners have difficulties understanding concepts because they lack the background knowledge and vocabulary that the curriculum requires. This problem is particularly prevalent for students who enter school without a good command of their native language.

BACKGROUND KNOWLEDGE AND ITS RELATIONSHIP WITH VOCABULARY

Ms. Torres's second-grade bilingual class was getting ready to go on a field trip to the Bronx Zoo. During the class meeting, she asked the students what animals they wanted to see. One

EL child raised her hand and said, "dogs and cats." The teacher did not respond and moved on to other students. When the class came back from the zoo, the teacher asked the children during a class meeting to tell her what they saw. The same girl responded with "no cats and no dogs." The teacher again ignored the response. Observing this interaction made us think that this student did not have the vocabulary in her background knowledge for the animals she saw in the zoo. No one gave her the words for those animals; therefore, her only frame of reference for animals was "cats and dogs." The student could not express the names of the zoo animals that she had seen for the first time, because she lacked the words to label animals like the elephant or the cheetah. The only thing that she could say was, "There were no cats and no dogs."

The learning experience for this child would have been much more positive if in-class preparation had been offered. For example, before the class trip the children could have spent some time looking at pictures and learning the names of the different animals they were going to see at the zoo, and talking about the characteristics of some of them. Without the words and this necessary preparation, this field experience was lost for this student.

This episode underlines the importance of connecting vocabulary with concepts and experience. We can expose our EL children to many rich experiences, but without connecting those experiences with their word meanings, a lot of the positive impact of the experience will be lost.

THE ROLE THAT BACKGROUND KNOWLEDGE PLAYS IN OUR LEARNING

Background knowledge is a frame of reference that we all have and that is indispensable in order to make sense of the world and to understand how it works; we have to rely on what we know in order to learn something new. For example, if we are studying the planets and we learn that Venus has a very poisonous atmosphere, the new information (Venus has a poisonous atmosphere) is built onto our knowledge that there are planets and Venus is one of them. Perhaps a student also knows of (or has seen) some poisonous cleaning substances at home and can relate the two concepts. Background knowledge is a reference base for our personal experiences, the accumulation of our lifelong learning, and our knowledge built from experience of what to expect in different situations (or *schema*) (Snow, 2007). For example, we know from our experience that the behavior and language we use in a birthday party will be different from the behavior and language we use in a classroom, just as the sequence of events will be different. We all depend on our life experiences and our internal schema to help us organize and anticipate events. Background knowledge is the relevant knowledge that we use to try to understand and organize new information.

The way that background knowledge works is by allowing us to compare new information against information that we already have in our heads (Snow et al., 2007). The listener (or reader) will compare the information, decide if it matches what she knows, and decide if it contains new elements (adding to our background knowledge) or if the new information requires that there be a shift in knowledge and that older elements be discarded. Without these processes, there is no learning. For example, let's assume that we believe, based on our own experiences, that being exposed to inclement weather will give us a cold. We then read a science article that explains that colds are produced by viruses and not by inclement weather. The new information moves us to compare our experience with what we read in the article and either accept the new information, adding this to our background knowledge, or reject it based on our past experiences. If we decide that our belief was wrong, then there will be a shift in our understanding of how colds are transmitted.

Schema

As we give our students new information, they are constantly measuring it against what they already know and adding to their repertoire, as long as there is some context to evaluate the new information. The problem for many EL and struggling students is that they do not have a background experience that matches the experiences that school requires, so they do not have the context.

We believe that every student arrives to school with a valuable set of experiences. Sometimes this experience does not match the experience of children born and educated in the Unites States, but it is equally precious and an important resource for teachers. For example, many students may have been exposed to civil strife and political turmoil in their native countries; this can be a valuable resource in social studies. Other students may have gone through the terrible experience of coming into this country as undocumented immigrants and have suffered the indignities of the passage; therefore, they understand the issues that immigrants face. Some students have experience with farming and know about plants and nature. It is very important for teachers to use those experiences as valuable resources for their teaching.

Background knowledge encompasses all the experiences, world knowledge, beliefs, and values that we have accumulated either through our experiences or through the experiences of others. This would include reading, talking, and watching carefully selected media, for example Animal Planet, the History Channel, documentaries, and a variety of nonfiction programs. Children who come to school without having been exposed to hearing stories read to them and without experiences with paper and pencil do not understand how reading and writing work (Cunningham & Allington, 2007); consequently they have different background knowledge than those children who have been exposed to books and pencil and paper from an early age. Background knowledge has a lot to do also with value systems; therefore, a child from a home where books and academic education are important would place more value on reading, while a child from a home where farming is the key experience would place more value on the natural sciences.

Our background knowledge is not only important because it represents what we know about the world, it also affects how we learn new information, how we store it, and how we remember it. In order to learn new information, we have to know where to place it in our minds. Does it remind us of something? Can we think of something similar? We need to understand how to frame the new information in relation to what we know, and how it connects with its associations. It is therefore indispensable to ask the students what they know about a topic or a story and, whenever possible, connect the reading to their experiences (Harvey, 1998; Marzano, 2004).

Getting Started: Triggering Background Knowledge

When we ask our students what they know about a topic before we begin teaching it, we are modeling a comprehension strategy. Good readers form certain expectations (or activate schema) by looking at the title of a story, book, or article; by skimming through the text and recognizing some words; by looking at the pictures or reading the subtitles. Even if the schema is very basic (meaning that we know very little about the subject), it becomes extremely helpful to use because we can organize the new information that we are learning.

We can facilitate the triggering of background knowledge by

- helping students connect new learning with their previous knowledge,
- using semantic webbing to help students make connections, and
- helping students organize the information.

Help students connect new learning with their previous knowledge

EL and struggling students often have some knowledge about a new topic that we are getting ready to teach, but they need help in connecting what they already know with the new information. We need to coach them to make the connections. When we explicitly link the student's past experiences with new concepts, we are building bridges to new understandings. There are several strategies that we can use to trigger background knowledge. When teaching a new concept, we can start by asking students what they already know about the subject using ***KWL charts*** (What I **K**now, What I **W**ant to Know, and What I **L**earned) (Ogle, 1986). Teachers use KWL charts to activate students' prior knowledge by asking them what they already know about a subject. Then, students work in small groups to decide what they want to learn. After researching information, students discuss in their group what they have learned and go back to their chart to describe their new learning.

Mary Serrano used the KWL chart in Figure 1.1 to teach her fifth-grade students to use text features to trigger background knowledge about a topic before they read a nonfiction text. Although Ms. Serrano's class is monolingual, seven students are ELs, and she knows she needs to provide very explicit support for these students as well as for the other struggling learners in her class. She gave her students explicit examples on how to "read" the title, headings, subheadings, and pictures; how to use the information to explore what they already know about the topic; and how to figure out what they may want to learn as they read the text.

KWL Chart

Figure 1.1   Sample KWL Chart

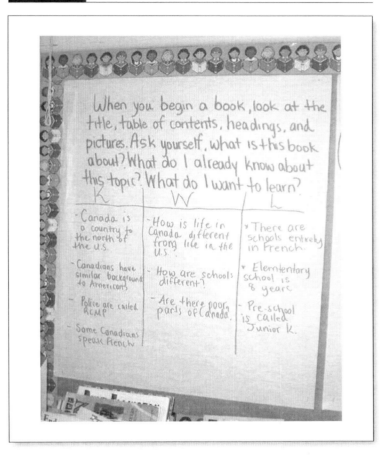

From Karen Schejtman.

She then divided the class into groups and provided each group with books on different topics. Students were asked to integrate into their prior thinking the information they gathered from looking at the text features, and to merge what they had learned with earlier information from other texts.

As the class was working on the assignment, the teacher pulled the EL and struggling students into a group and scaffolded the assignment by showing them several examples of nonfiction books about Canada. Ms. Serrano asked them to describe what they noticed. Some students noticed the captions and pictures, while others noticed the headings and subheadings. She then provided a chart where the children listed what they had learned about nonfiction books. As a second step, she asked the children to list what they may find out about the book if they look at the pictures, headings, and subheadings. Students worked in groups, jotting down the information they had found (see Table 1.2).

Table 1.2   What I Learned About Nonfiction Books

What I Noticed About Nonfiction Books	What I May Learn About a Nonfiction Book by Looking
• Nonfiction texts have headings, subheadings • They also may have pictures	• The headings may tell me what the book is all about • The subheadings and pictures will give me more information

Ms. Serrano then asked the students to think about what they already knew about the topic and what they wanted to learn by asking leading questions such as *"Can you figure out what this book is about just by looking at the headings and subheadings?"* and *"Does looking at these features make you think about information you may have already about the topic?"* She carefully chose books that did not have **language overload**, meaning that there was picture support with clear captions under each picture. The language was clear.

At the end of this process, the children were able to complete the same task that the rest of the class had done with the KWL chart.

Language Overload

Use *semantic maps* to help students *create connections*

Semantic maps

Semantic maps help students clarify their ideas before they read or discuss a new topic. We create "semantic maps" with the topic positioned in the center and students' responses about their related experience placed around it. Semantic maps offer a good way to engage students in the topic and to find out what they already know.

Ms. Serrano always begins new units by asking her students what they want to learn about a particular topic. She starts with a general introduction, such as *"What do you know about . . . ?"* in order to find out what the children already know. Through the vocabulary they use, she can test how deep their understanding is.

The teacher is very careful to allow the children to make free associations. Figure 1.3 shows an example of how a group of her students described what they knew about spiders.

Help the students to organize the information

Table 1.4 shows how Ms. Serrano's students categorized the information.

When children are writing an informational book, or when the class is studying a specific topic, helping them to build a semantic map, organizing what they already know, clarifies their thinking and provides opportunities for focused research on the topic. At the end of the unit, they can go back to their original map and add the new knowledge they have acquired. What one group of Ms. Serrano's children produced can be seen in Figure 1.5.

Background Knowledge and Vocabulary

As children are exposed to new ideas, their background knowledge is constantly changing, and their repertoire of words connected to the new learning is growing. The role of vocabulary in learning and in advancing background knowledge is key to understanding. For example, let's assume that a child doesn't know how to ride a bicycle, but she knows what a bicycle is. The

Figure 1.3 Semantic Map of *Spiders*

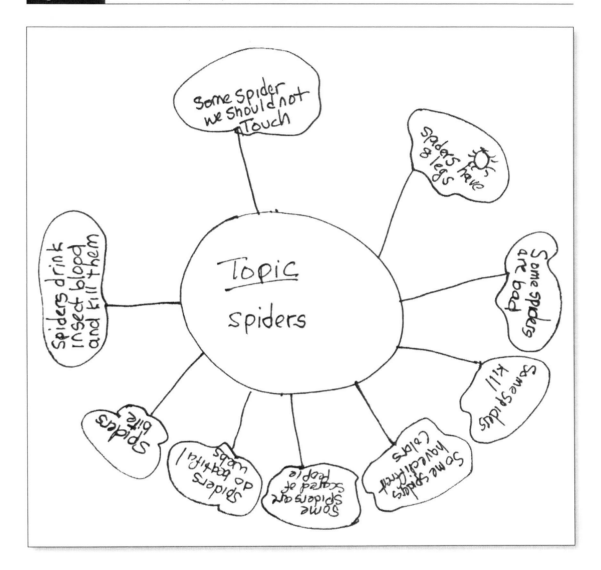

Table 1.4 How Ms. Serrano's Students Categorized the Information About Spiders

Physical Characteristics of Spiders	How People Feel About Spiders
• Several legs • Can be big • What do they eat? • Trap other insects	• Scared • They are ugly • Some bite

child also knows what a pedal is. As soon as she learns how to ride a bicycle, she will learn more words that reflect her experience with the bicycle. *Balance* and *swerving* might be words she didn't know, but as she experiences riding a bike, she understand the process and incorporate these words into her background knowledge.

Figure 1.5 Semantic Map of *Spiders* After More Information Has Been Added

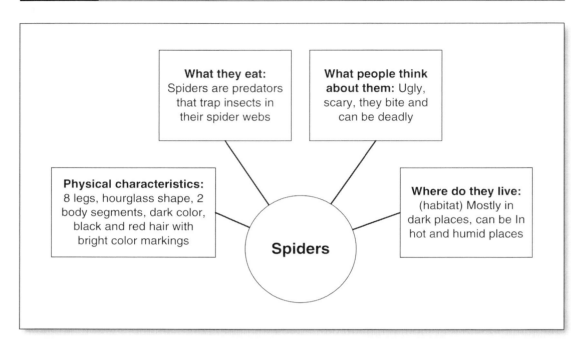

Background knowledge is deeply intertwined with vocabulary. We express our knowledge through vocabulary (Marzano, 2004). However, as many teachers of EL students know, vocabulary is one of the main areas where second language learners lag behind. This is particularly relevant if they come from families with low literacy backgrounds. Their academic vocabulary in their first and second language might be limited.

Vocabulary is the body of words we know and their meanings (Graves, 2005). Throughout our lives we continuously expand our knowledge of vocabulary. As our reading expands and our conversations acquire more depth, our knowledge of vocabulary increases.

When students are taught vocabulary in a thorough fashion, their reading comprehension should improve. EL and struggling students develop knowledge of vocabulary through conversations and through extensive reading of engaging texts that are rich in new words. In addition, vocabulary can be increased through explicit teaching. By this, we don't mean providing students with extensive lists of words and definitions that have to be memorized. William Nagy (1988) demonstrated that looking for definitions of words in the dictionary and memorizing them does not increase vocabulary. The most effective way to develop vocabulary is through activating the child's background knowledge and helping the child make connections to other words through reading experiences. A focus on language development and enrichment has to permeate all aspects of the curriculum that is presented to second language learners.

The most effective way to enrich the language of our students is by creating a classroom environment full of words (Blachowicz & Cobb, 2007). If we want our EL students to develop a rich vocabulary, these are the things we should do:

- Do an *interactive read aloud* at least once a day, taking time to pinpoint new words, giving definitions *on the run.*
- Stop and discuss the meaning of words throughout the day.

[handwritten margin notes: "Vocabulary Definition", "Explicit Vocabulary Instruction"]

- Label different objects in the classroom.
- Provide puzzles, riddles, and word games, and entice the children to use them during free periods of the day.
- Take every opportunity to expand vocabulary. For example, if we are going to take children on a field trip to the zoo, then time should be spent on "zoo-related" vocabulary, for example, *species*, *mammals*, *reptiles*, *vertebrates*, *invertebrates*.
- Take time to teach new words within the context of our lessons, on a daily basis.
  - Have *word walls* that reflect student input.
  - Ask students to write new words in *word journals* (or writer's journals where students keep their notes, write drafts, and make diary entries. A specific section of the notebook can be devoted to new words).

Vocabulary is learned through context and in everyday situations. Spending time during our classroom conversations focusing on words and their meanings is important for our students' learning process.

Ms. Annelli is a bilingual, second-grade teacher. She has always been very interested in finding new ways to develop vocabulary. During independent reading, Ms. Annelli organized her second graders in groups of four. Each group has a box of index cards, and every time a child reads a word that he or she cannot understand, students write the word on an index card. When Ms. Annelli confers with each group of students, she pulls the cards from the box and reads the words, asking the children if they know the meaning. If they do not, she gives *explanations on the run.* This means she explains the word at that moment. For example, she says, "A *cabin* is a house made of wood and located in rural areas. Abraham Lincoln lived in a cabin." She only works with four words at a time and spends a few minutes of the conference doing this. Children then write the words in their word journals. This activity is successful because the words are self-selected and are discussed in the context of the students' reading.

The most effective tool to increase vocabulary and develop the language of ELs and struggling students is the language that the teacher uses in everyday classroom life because students always try to emulate their teacher. We saw this by observing Ms. Roberts with her third graders. The teacher was very depressed a day after her dog died. When her third-grade students asked why she was sad, she told them she was feeling *miserable* and *melancholy*. She missed her dog very much. The words *miserable* and *melancholy* were words the students had never heard before. The next day, one of her kids was downcast. Ms. Roberts asked, "What is the matter?" The student responded, "I feel miserable. I have a cold." Later on that day, we heard a student say, "I feel melancholy because my best friend didn't come to school." Even though in this case, the student was not using the word exactly as it should be used, we know that she got the idea of what *melancholy* meant. Teachers offer the best language models for their EL students as the children often do not have good English linguistic models outside of school.

Different Kinds of Vocabulary

For many EL children, the lack of academic vocabulary and conceptual knowledge in their native language has a direct impact on how they perform in English-speaking classrooms—their lack of understanding and participation in classroom activities grows exponentially as they move up in the grades, with dire consequences for their future. When EL children have good command of their native language and good conceptual knowledge, their chances of academic success increase.

Some EL children are at a clear disadvantage when they enter school. It is easier for a native English-speaking child to learn the meaning of a new word if he knows related words and concepts in English. When EL children lack those related words, they begin to miss out on information the teacher is giving out, and their alienation grows with time. Many struggling English-dominant students have the same issues. English-speaking children who come with good vocabulary listen to stories, learn more words, feel confident, and their vocabulary continues growing with their conceptual knowledge development (Hart & Risley, 2003).

EL children who arrive in school with a rich native-language vocabulary adapt very easily to the new language, and their conceptual knowledge continues to grow as their English vocabulary expands. However, EL children who come to school with poor vocabulary and conceptual knowledge in their native language have a hard time following the lesson because they don't have concepts to refer to in their native language; therefore, they miss out on the meaning of the lesson and fall further behind.

When EL children who have not been exposed to academic vocabulary in their native language move into upper elementary grades, middle school, and high school, they often lack the required vocabulary to tackle difficult texts (August, Carlo, Dressler, & Snow, 2005). Many of these students lack the vocabulary to comprehend content-area texts, since that kind of vocabulary is more specialized and requires prior exposure. These learners, along with many of their native English-speaking classmates, require thoughtful, targeted instruction in academic English vocabulary.

Decide what words you are going to teach

When we think about teaching vocabulary, we need to decide the words we want our students to learn, why we are choosing these words, and how we are going to teach them. Unless we have a framework for what is important for the children to know, we end up just throwing words at random at our students.

Not all vocabulary is the same. Vocabulary experts usually group words into different categories. Usually the categories reflect the fact that there are some words that children will learn from their environment or from their interactions. These are the everyday useful words that are part of social language. There are some words that go across the curriculum, which children will encounter in their academic setting across the subject areas. Finally, there are technical words that correspond to specific content-area domains.

Beck, McKeown, and Kucan (2005) divide vocabulary into three tiers:

Tier 1 includes basic words that are learned without explicit instruction or attention because they refer to everyday situations and interactions—for example, *chair*, *pencil*, *food*, *walk*, and *run*. For EL students, many of these are words they know in their native language. It also includes words that are easy to describe (if students do not know them) or easy to show visuals to create the concept of what they mean. These words usually appear in beginning-level reading books. Words such as *clock*, *baby*, and *milk* are Tier 1 words.

Tier 2 consists of words that are frequently and commonly used across many contents and domains but that may require explicit teaching because they are not part of everyday interactions. These words are often part of our academic discourse. Coxhead (2000) analyzed a series of texts from different disciplines. She came up with an Academic Word List (website: www.uefap.com/vocab/select/awl.htm). This list presents 10 sublists of words according to frequency of occurrence in academic texts. As an example, Sublist 1 words are those that are most commonly used, and Sublist 10 contains words that are less frequently used. Knowing these words is useful because they can be found in a multitude of subject areas. Once a student knows the meaning of one of these words, he will encounter them repeatedly in different contexts. For example, the word *analysis* can be found in history, math, English, and social studies texts. Coxhead's Academic Word List corresponds to what Beck et al. (2005) define as Tier 2 words. For EL students, Tier 2 words are harder words to learn. Words such as *discuss*, *retell*, and *confront* fall within this category. Many Tier 2 words have an associated word in Tier 1—*discuss*, for example, can be associated with *talk about*, a Tier 1 concept. According to Beck et al., students may already have a concept of what Tier 2 words mean, making it easier for them to learn the words through their simpler synonyms. When a student knows a Tier 1 word, you can expand his vocabulary by introducing its Tier 2 equivalent. For example, the student may know the meaning of *upset*, and you can use that to teach him the meaning of *distress*.

Tier 3 includes words that are technical and connected to the content areas, such as *peninsula*, *plateau*, *revolution*, *refinery*, and *isotope*.

[handwritten margin note: Technical words specific to content-area domains]

Understanding how vocabulary differs can help us target academic language development more effectively and decide what words to teach and when to teach them. In our lessons we can use the children's previous knowledge as building blocks for the acquisition of new words. If EL students do not know the basic words, we need to teach those first, and then build upon them to move into academic language.

Build vocabulary by connecting Tier 1 words with Tier 2 words

For EL and struggling students, building on the words and concepts they already have to develop a more sophisticated vocabulary provides the scaffolding they need to continue to expand their language. An example from a third-grade class follows.

Ms. Martinez put the paragraph shown in Figure 1.6 on an overhead projector during shared reading. Shared reading is described in detail in Chapter 3. It is a structure that allows students to read a short passage with a specific purpose (i.e., fluency, conventions, etc.). In this case, the shared reading was used to teach vocabulary. Ms. Martinez covered the Tier 2 words with sticky notes containing Tier 1 words and asked her students to come up with equivalent words from the context.

[handwritten margin note: Shared Reading purposes: • fluency • conventions • vocabulary]

Figure 1.6 Covering Tier 2 With Tier 1 Words in a Paragraph

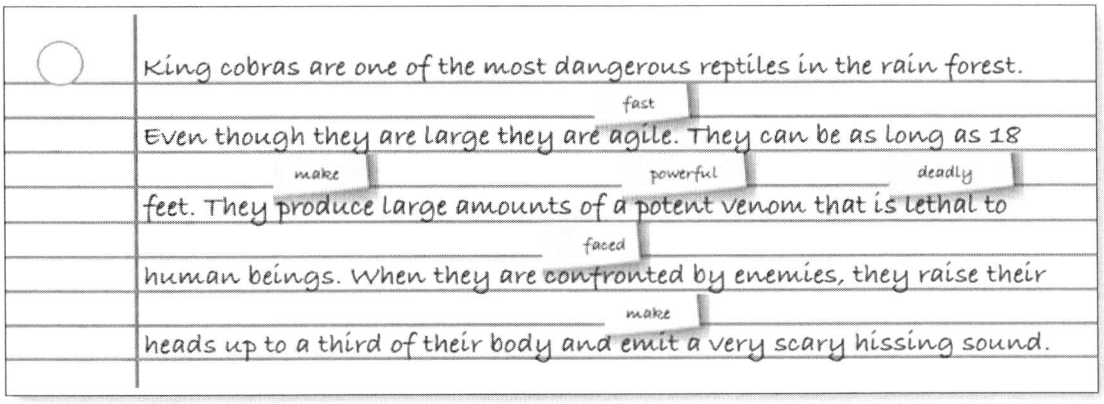

King cobras are one of the most dangerous reptiles in the rain forest.
Even though they are large they are agile. *[fast]* They can be as long as 18
feet. They produce large amounts of a potent venom that is lethal to *[make] [powerful] [deadly]*
human beings. When they are confronted by enemies, they raise their *[faced]*
heads up to a third of their body and emit a very scary hissing sound. *[make]*

Table 1.7 Tier 1 and Tier 2 Words

Tier 1	Tier 2
fast	agile
make	produce
powerful	potent
deadly	lethal
faced	confronted
make	emit

Figure 1.8 Teaching a Tier 2 Word Using a Tier 1 Word

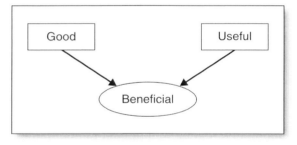

Figure 1.9 Connecting Tier 1 and Tier 3 Words

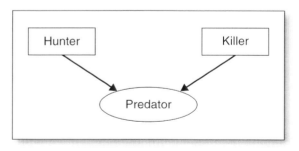

The students and the teacher read the text and tried to figure out the equivalent word underneath the sticky note. When they were not able to discover the word, they came to the board and raised the note. After this exercise, they connected the Tier 1 words with the Tier 2 words (Table 1.7).

Studies show that words should be processed repeatedly and deeply and that students typically learn words gradually through immersion in a word-rich environment and involvement in fun word activities. Furthermore, we don't learn words through definitions. We learn them by association with similar words.

Figure 1.8 provides an example of how we would teach a Tier 2 word using a Tier 1 word that the children already know. The new (Tier 2) word is *beneficial*.

In the web seen in Figure 1.9, we are helping students learn a Tier 3 word (*predator*) by using Tier 1 words. This is the way we learn words—by storing them in a web of related words. We store them when we use them. The following strategy tackles both things: the web where we can understand words and a technique for using the word in order to store it.

The best way to ensure that children will incorporate new words into their repertoire is by providing them with opportunities to use them, by listening to them, and by prompting the children to use them during classroom discussions.

Teachers often ask us how many new words they should add to their students' repertoire during the course of a week. Our advice is to start slowly, but much depends on the needs of the curriculum. Words should not be taught out of context. You may start by picking the two or three most important words for your lesson, and then you can build it up to five or eight. Having lists of 100 words per week will not be productive for your students since they will have time neither to use them nor to store them in their long-term memory. Choose words children will use during the week. This is the main element for success.

Get children to add the new words to their repertoire in fun ways

A great way to challenge the kids to incorporate the words into their repertoire is by asking them to use the new words as many times as they can in their daily life. Invite them to use the words at least 20 times during the course of a week. They can put tally marks on a chart where you have written the words.

Ms. Serrano improved on this strategy not only by putting tally marks on the words in the chart but by having the children add their initials (see Figure 1.10). This let the children see who had used the new words and increased their interest in using them.

Figure 1.10   Interactive Word Wall

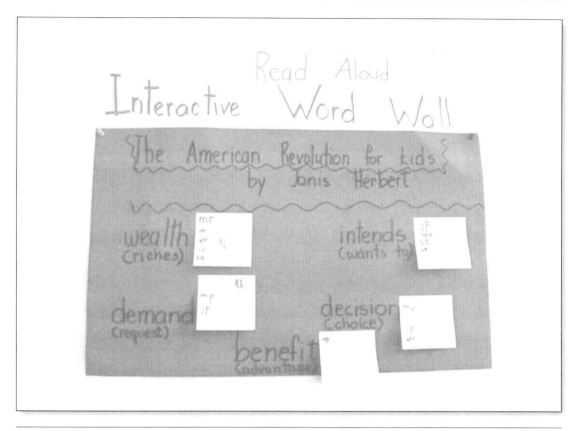

Note: The sticky notes are notes from students indicating how many times they have used the individual words.

Use graphic organizers to connect concepts to vocabulary

One way for teachers to immerse students in the vocabulary and language structures from the unit of study is to build a word-rich environment in their classroom with the key words and structures the students are expected to use throughout the month. Some teachers have *word walls* for particular content areas and ask students to keep their own vocabulary notebooks. Other teachers use specific graphic organizers to connect concepts with vocabulary, posting well-known organizers such as ***concept definition maps*** (Buehl, 2009) and ***word sorts*** (Echevarria, Vogt, & Short, 2000) around the room. Following is a description and example (Figure 1.11) of a concept definition map and a word sort (Figure 1.12).

Concept Definition Map

1. Choose a word or concept that relates to the topic being studied and write it in the center of the graphic organizer. Keep in mind a few questions:
   o What is the central word, concept, research question, or problem around which to build the map? For example: *revolution.*
   o What are the concepts? The items, descriptive words, or telling questions that you can associate with the concept?

[handwritten margin notes:]
★ Word walls
★ vocabulary notebooks
★ graphic organizers
— Concept definition maps
— word sorts

Figure 1.11 Concept Definition Map

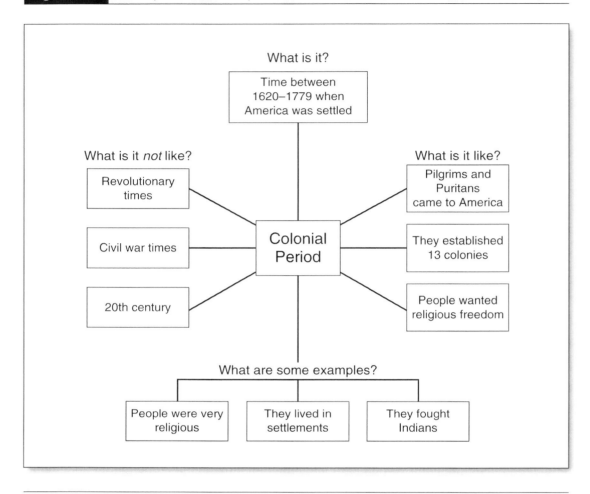

Source: Buehl (2009, p. 41).

2. Explain to the students that to understand new vocabulary, they need to know what makes up the definition of a word. To do this, they have to answer three questions:
   ○ What is it? (Category)
   ○ What is it like? (Properties) *and* not *like*
   ○ What are some examples?

Word Sorts

Word sorts are activities in which the teacher defines the process for categorizing the words (Echeverria et al., 2000). This requires students to engage in critical thinking as they examine the vocabulary, corresponding concepts, or word structure (see Figure 1.12).

Golden Rules of Vocabulary Teaching

- Teach in context. Words that are taught in isolation are not stored in long-term memory and, therefore, are quickly forgotten.
- Think of related words that connect to the word, e.g., *sad—melancholy—blue*.
- Give the opposite of the word so as to throw light on the meaning of the target word, e.g., *melancholy—happy*.
- Make a personal connection—get the children to incorporate the word into their repertoire and start using it.
- Use the word repeatedly!

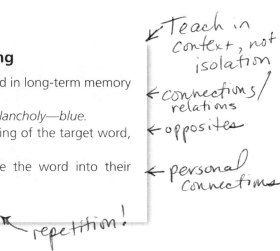

Teach in context, not isolation

← connections/ relations

← opposites

← personal connections

← repetition!

Figure 1.12 Word Sorts

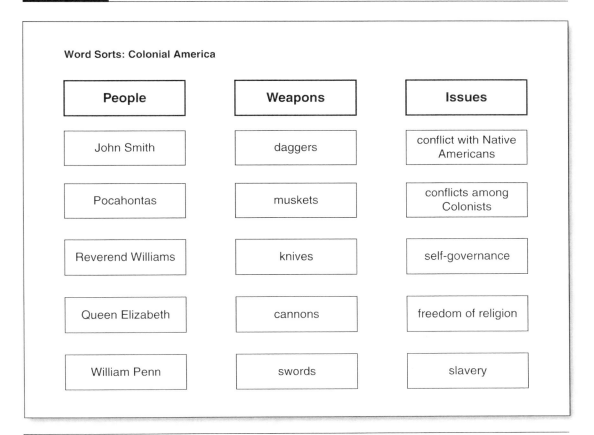

Word Sorts: Colonial America

People	Weapons	Issues
John Smith	daggers	conflict with Native Americans
Pocahontas	muskets	conflicts among Colonists
Reverend Williams	knives	self-governance
Queen Elizabeth	cannons	freedom of religion
William Penn	swords	slavery

Source: Based on Echevarria, Vogt, and Short (2000, p. 65).

Use cognates as a strategy for learning words

Cognates are words that share the same linguistic roots; this means that they look very similar in written language. Spanish and English have Latin, Greek, and Sanskrit as their common ancestors; therefore, many words have retained the same roots. An example of cognates between English and Spanish would be the words *revolution* and *revolución*. Both words have very similar spelling and mean the same. Many teachers who have Spanish-speaking ELs in their classrooms overlook the teaching of cognates as a strategy for the development of vocabulary and background knowledge, but this could be a great resource for activating students' prior knowledge and conceptual knowledge. Researchers say that about two-thirds of the words between Spanish and English are cognates (Snow, 2005). Making the connection between the cognates in Spanish and English is a powerful strategy for learning new words. Cognates are present with more frequency in nonfiction texts. The more demanding the text, the more cognates we will find. Here are some examples of cognates found in English and Spanish: *map—mapa, elevator—elevador, animal—animal, independence—independencia.* A small number of cognates are referred to as "false cognates" because even though the words in English and Spanish look the same; the meanings are completely different. A very well-known example is *embarrassed/embarazada*—the English word means *uncomfortable* and the Spanish word means *pregnant*.

You can use cognates in the classroom by *frontloading* (preteaching) the cognates as a way to trigger background knowledge. This will help the students to develop a framework to approach the new information. Another useful way of using cognates is by engaging the children in finding cognates in a text and encouraging them to "discover" the meaning.

MORPHOLOGY AND SYNTAX

Language Acquisition Versus Language Learning

As we visit classrooms, we have observed that teachers tend to spend a lot of time during the writing workshop encouraging children to focus on ideas, working on multiple drafts, and revising and publishing their pieces. They spend much less time helping children to edit their pieces, taking into account grammar, punctuation, spelling, and vocabulary. This means that EL students seldom get the chance to address language difficulties, which then linger throughout their schooling.

Many of the teachers we work with are often conflicted about teaching grammatical structures to their EL children. They do not know how to strike a balance between allowing children to acquire their second language naturally, through classroom interactions and general exposure to the language, and teaching them appropriate syntactic structures. Krashen (1997) makes a distinction between language learning and language acquisition. Language acquisition means children are learning the second language naturally, through speaking and listening in meaningful interactions and through reading and writing. We all learn our first language in such a way. Language learning, on the other hand, is the conscious understanding of grammatical rules, and it comes as a result of explicit instruction.

Teachers stay away from explicit teaching of language structures because they have a hard time figuring out when to teach or what to teach. The timing for explicit language instruction is an issue. Children who are at the early stages of language acquisition need to experiment with language, speaking and listening, and would probably do better without much explicit language instruction, as they cannot integrate grammar rules at this point. The most important goal for beginner speakers of any language is to communicate and get their message across. On the other hand, children who are at the later stages of language acquisition do need some explicit language instruction. As children move up in the grades, they encounter texts that use complex sentence structures that they may have a hard time understanding or using in their writing.

In the following section, we will illustrate the types of difficulties that EL and struggling children encounter when dealing with words, complex sentences, and pronoun substitutions and describe strategies to help students master them.

morphology - studies words (smallest units that express meaning)
— independent/free (words)
— bound morphemes (prefixes/suffixes)

BUILDING LANGUAGE **19**

Improving comprehension of morphology and sentence patterns (syntax)

Morphology is the area of linguistics that studies words. These are the smallest units that express meaning (Fillmore & Snow, 2000). There are two kinds of morphemes: independent or free morphemes, which essentially refer to any word; and bound morphemes, which have to be attached to another word (or independent morpheme). These can be prefixes or suffixes, and they modify the meaning of the word. Examples of bound morphemes are the use of /s/ as a plural marker (house/houses), *ing* at the end of a verb (build/building), and *ly* and *ness* to form adverbs and nouns (happily and happiness).

Syntax studies how words are organized into complete sentences (Altenberg & Vago, 2010). Syntax refers to the order of words and to the agreement between the words in a sentence (such as subject-verb agreement, verb tense, and number). When we discuss syntax, we are referring to the set of rules that govern the structure of sentences in a language. Most of the rules are acquired naturally as children develop language through meaningful experiences and interactions. There are some grammatical structures, however, such as complex sentence patterns, that will require explicit instruction for children to understand them. By explicit instruction, we do not mean drills but, rather, helping children to recognize these structures and giving them strategies to process them.

Syntax - how words are organized — word order — agreement

← defn.

Ms. Alvarez was very concerned about the writing of her sixth graders. Most of her language arts class was composed of second language learners at different stages of language acquisition, but even children who had been in the school system for their entire schooling were still writing in short sentences and making a lot of mistakes. Ms. Alvarez said, *"Their sentences are unfinished and very simple. Sometimes, the verbs used are in the past tense and in the next line the verbs will be in the present tense. The /s/ as a plural marker is absent in many nouns that are clearly plural. The students get how to develop a character, how to write a dialogue, but are struggling with the quality of the writing."*

We pointed out to Ms. Alvarez that all these elements are related to syntax and morphology. The teacher was upset because she had spent a considerable amount of time going over language rules, but it was not having an impact on the quality of the students' writing.

After our discussions, the teacher tried a new strategy to help the students internalize the rules:

1. She placed a sample of student writing on an overhead, side by side with the same piece written in a syntactically correct form (see Table 1.13).

2. She asked the students to work in pairs, comparing the two pieces and highlighting the differences.

✶ Compare Writing Samples

Table 1.13 Student Version Compared to Correct Version

Student Version	Correct Version
Hispanic peoples also play a part in Buffalo diversity. In 1990, about 16,000 hispanic peoples live in Buffalo. In 2000 more than 22,000 live in the city. They mainly live in the Lower East Side. The Lower east Side is the Hispanic center of the city. The first immigrant groups to come were from Mexico and Puerto Rico and they worked mostly in the canneri and farms outside of the city and in the fatory and mill inside the city.	Hispanic people also played a part in Buffalo's diversity. In 1990, about 16,000 Hispanic people lived in Buffalo. In 2000 more than 22,000 lived in the city. They mainly lived in the Lower East Side, which is the Hispanic center of the city. The first immigrant groups to come were from Mexico and Puerto Rico, and they worked mostly in the canneries and farms outside of the city and in the factories and mills inside of the city.

3. She read the correct version before the one that the student had written.

4. The students worked in pairs to figure out which version was better.

5. The children then shared their findings.

Here are some examples of the discussion that ensued:

Martin   I noticed that Hispanic people lived in the city. It has a *d* because it is the past tense.

Gloria   I also noticed that Hispanic is written with a capital *H*.

Roberto   I noticed that you put two sentences together: "They mainly lived in the Lower East Side, which is the Hispanic center of the city" instead of "They mainly live in the Lower East Side. The Lower East Side is . . . ."

The discussion continued for a while, as children discussed other mistakes they found in the student sample. After the discussion, the teacher categorized the kinds of mistakes the children found and spent some time doing some explicit teaching within the context of the student sample. She focused on:

- past tense in verbs,
- plurals, and
- relative clauses.

During this exercise, the children had the opportunity to figure out how to apply the right syntax rules by comparing one text with the other. After the exercise, the teacher hung the two texts side by side on chart paper, and this worked as a scaffold for the kids. She continued doing this activity with texts of increasing difficulty, posting new examples as she took down the old ones and teaching new rules as they came up. The students used the charts frequently, going back over their mistakes; as a result, their writing improved dramatically. This activity offers us an example of how children can better learn rules of syntax in context.

Just as Ms. Alvarez pointed out, teachers often tell us that their upper grade EL and struggling students have a hard time using long sentences and pronouns properly in their writing. Although we know that children often read at a higher level than what we see in their writing, we find that the teachers have good reason to worry about their student's writing skills. One of the common denominators that we see in the writing of upper elementary EL and struggling children is the overuse of simple sentence patterns, rather than more complex sentences. The following writing sample is from a fourth-grade EL student who has been in the United States for 4 years:

The Duch, English, and French colonists were the most important groups in New York State. The Duch were the oreginal group. in New York. They still were very influential. In Albany most of the buildings were in Duch style. The buildings had gabelss and made of brik.

The challenge for teachers is to find ways to teach complex sentence constructions that students can understand clearly and integrate into their repertoire. Mastering complex syntactic structures is a key element in mastering academic language.

Ms. Martinez asked her students to work in pairs combining some of the sentences in the above example. First, she modeled what she meant. Then, she showed the two versions side by side, asking her children which one sounded better (see Table 1.14). Students felt Ms. Martinez's version was better.

Table 1.14   Student Version and Ms. Martinez's Version

Student Version	Ms. Martinez's Version
The Duch, English, and French colonists were the most important groups in New York State. The Duch were the oreginal group. in New York. They still were very influential.	The Dutch, English, and French were the most important groups in New York State. **The Dutch were the original group, and they were very influential.**

This exercise also allowed children to correct misspellings. Here are some examples of the first attempts at sentence combining by the students:

The Dutch were the original group in New York, and they still were very influential.

The Dutch, English, and French were the most important groups in New York State; the Dutch were the original group, and they were very influential.

Later on, the children worked on rewriting the entire paragraph:

The Dutch, English, and French colonists were the most important groups in New York State, but the Dutch were the original group in New York; they lost to the British but they still were very influential. In Albany most of the buildings were in Dutch style, they had gables and were made of brick.

The next step in this process was engaging the students in using ***connectives*** (or conjunctions) in addition to *and* and *but*, which are used too frequently.
Ms. Martinez left a blank space where the connectives should be. She also gave the children a list of options, and they had to decide if a connective made sense or not. The students tried several options and finally decided that *however* and *although* were the best conjunctions for this paragraph.

The Dutch, English, and French colonists were the most important groups in New York State, _____ the Dutch were the original group in New York; they lost to the British _____ they still were very influential. In Albany most of the buildings were in Dutch style, they had gables and were made of brick.

Options to Try in the Blank Spaces

- before
- although
- unless
- however

✗ option bank

We use connectives (or signal words) to show the relationship between sentences (see Table 1.15). The connectives can change the meaning of the sentence. For example:

The soldiers were anxious but they were quiet.
The soldiers were anxious therefore they were quiet.

Table 1.15   Different Connectives

Cause and Effect	Comparing and Contrasting	Conclusions or Summaries	Arranging Ideas in Time	Changing Direction or Reversing Action
therefore, because, since, so that, thus, as a result	like, although, even though, though, however, but, on the contrary, yet, otherwise, on the other hand	Consequently, therefore, thus, hence, accordingly	until, meanwhile, always, finally, during, initially, first, then, after, as, before, since, when, whenever	However, not, yet, but, instead

Relative clauses

Relative clauses are very confusing for EL students because two actions are happening simultaneously. These types of syntactic constructions require that two sentences (independent clause and dependent clause) are comprehended separately and yet one depends on the other, for example, *"The soldiers were killed by cannon fire that came from behind the trees. The two clauses would be: 1) The soldiers were killed by cannon fire. 2) The cannon fire came from behind the trees."*

Many times the children read the first and last part of the sentence without processing the middle part. They would understand this sentence as *"the soldiers came from behind the trees."* Separating the sentences helps the children understand the subject of the relative clause. Once they are able to do this, we teach them to put the clauses back together. Here we are teaching them a strategy that they can use independently. The dependent clause is usually introduced by *that*, *who*, or *which*.

Letting Kids' Writing Guide Our Teaching

As students move up in the grades, they often are aware that their grammar and vocabulary fall short of their own expectations, and they may try to master some of the structures on their own. They may have noticed a pattern in the materials they are reading or in the language that their friends use. Looking for patterns in a student's writing may give us a good idea of his readiness to learn specific grammatical structures. The student is showing the way to his own "zone of proximal development" (Vygotsky & Cole, 1978); he is telling us what he is ready to learn.

We can see an example of this in Kevin's writing:

[handwritten margin notes: # Separate the 2 clauses, Understand the Subject, put the clauses back together]

[handwritten margin note: Zone of Proximal Development]

Baseball

During my summer vacation I paly basaball with my mon and my dad and my borither. I hit a home ran. I help my borither to playå basaball and my barither hit the ball in the graon. My borither ran fast than a car. He was fastr. My dad hit the ball than he have a home ran. My mom was have a got time in the park. I want home wath my dad, mom and my barither. I have a got time to eat lunch to rest I want to take a bath.

This example tells us where we should take Kevin next. Even though there are many grammatical, punctuation, and spelling mistakes, there was a clear message in his writing: He was attempting to master a comparative structure. He tried to use a comparative sentence pattern two times:

1. *My borither ran fast than a car.*
2. *He was fastr.*

Small-group work or a conference is the perfect structure to support Kevin in mastering a structure that he is clearly interested in. Taking the time to analyze his writing provides the teacher with a road map of where to take Kevin next.

Comprehending Pronoun Substitutions (Anaphoras)

Pronouns stand in the place of a noun. Table 1.16 shows different types of pronouns.

Table 1.16   Pronouns

Personal	Objective	Possessive	Demonstrative	Indefinite	Relative and Interrogative
I, you, he, she, it, etc.	me, you, him, her, etc.	my, mine, your, yours, theirs, etc.	this, that, these, those, etc.	each, any, anybody, either, neither, etc.	who, whom, whose, when, where, why, etc.

In order to process and understand what a pronoun is referring to, we need to process the previous (or, in some cases, the following) sentences, for example, *The Pilgrims were looking for religious freedom.* **They** *came to America to find* **it.**

They is substituting for *the pilgrims*, and *it* is referring to *freedom*. This kind of substitution is also referred as an **anaphora**.

EL and struggling students often get confused by pronouns because they have a hard time figuring out what the pronoun is referring to. Patricia was working with Tomás (a fifth grader) during reading time. When she asked him to summarize what he had read, she was surprised by how inaccurate he was.

Here is the passage that Tomás was reading:

My grandmother moved to our house when I was 6 years old. I remember her sitting by the front porch watching us play in the yard. She always wore a shawl around her shoulders because she was cold, even in the summer. My sister and I liked to run circles around her when she came out of the house. We always tried to confuse her. This got her upset. Grandma got angry and yelled at us. Once we made her fall and she got hurt. We were very sorry.

Tomás's summary was,

"The grandmother wore a shawl and she ran in circles."

When Patricia asked him to reread the section his frustration grew, and he asked her to make the summary for him. After she did it, he asked, "How do you know who did what? I can't figure it out." Patricia saw then that Tomás was very confused by the pronouns. He needed to understand how to use them in order to understand the text. Patricia used what Kylene Beers (2003) calls *syntactic surgery*; Tomás had to connect the pronouns with the nouns they replaced by an arrow (see Figure 1.17).

Figure 1.17   Sample of Syntactic Surgery

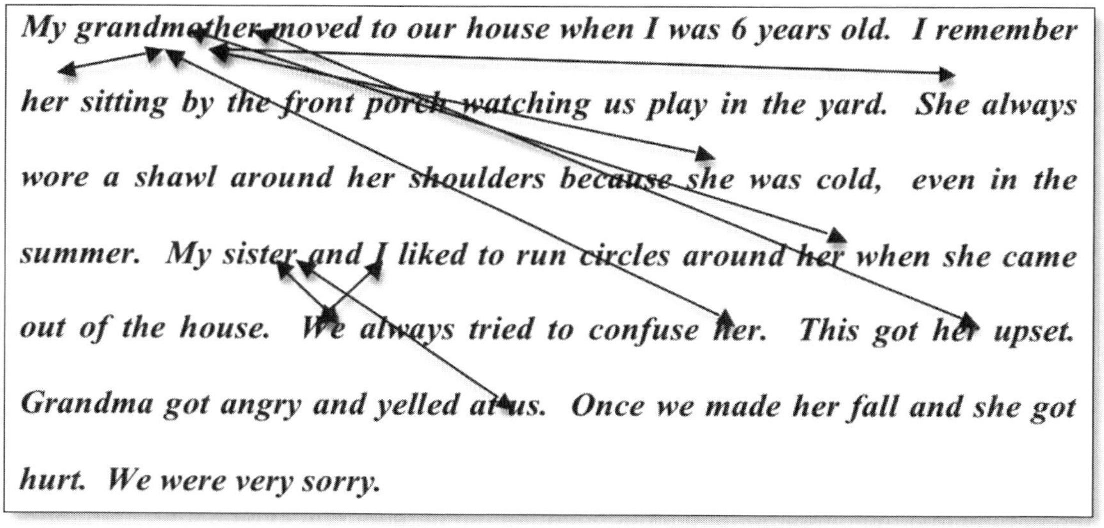

After connecting the nouns with the pronouns, Tomás had a much easier time figuring out the meaning of the text. The exercise taught this student that when he is confused, he needs to go back and draw an imaginary arrow connecting the noun with the pronoun.

Anaphoras not only substitute for a noun (as in the previous example); they can also substitute for a verb or even a whole sentence—for example, *My sister and I liked to run circles around her when she came out of the house. We always tried to confuse her.* **This** *got her upset.* **This** is substituting for the previous sentence.

FIGURATIVE LANGUAGE

In figurative language, we use images that are not supposed to be interpreted literally: *"He is as tall as a giraffe."* Some forms of figurative language you may be teaching the children are similes and metaphors.

Similes are comparisons between two things using *like*, *as*, or *than*. For example, "He was *as* quiet *as* a ghost." Most children enjoy working with similes, and it is much easier to introduce them to this figure of speech before we move to ***metaphors***, which are harder to understand. Metaphors are not introduced by comparative words such as *like* and *as*. Furthermore, metaphors are not explicit in terms of how the comparison is to be understood. In *he was quiet as a ghost*, *quiet* is the word that ties *he* and *ghost*. In the metaphor *he was a ghost*, the reader has to infer or interpret what is the common element that underlies the metaphor.

In Ms. Martinez's fourth-grade class, the teacher started by getting several sentence strips and making the middle of the similes *like*, *as*, and *than*. Then, she explained to the children that similes are sentences that make comparisons between two things. Next, she drew a web (see Figure 1.18) with an adjective in the middle and asked the children to think of tall objects or animals.

Figure 1.18 Simile Exercise

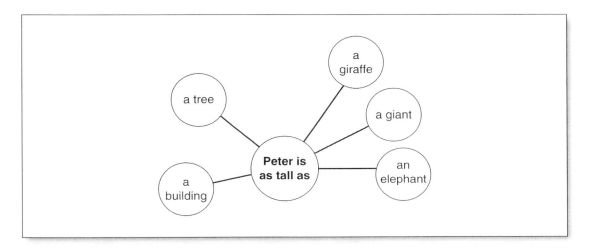

Ms. Martinez then asked her students to work in groups using similes with their partner's names and characteristics: *"Juan is as slow as a turtle; Jessica's desk is as dirty as garbage pail."* Children had a lot of fun with this activity. For the next step, the teacher asked students to find similes in the books they were reading.

Metaphors have a higher level of complexity because they do not use comparative words. After working with similes, Ms. Martinez decided to start teaching metaphors by asking children to convert similes to metaphors. The same similes that the students had previously created became the metaphors:

> *Juan is a turtle*
> *He is a ghost.*
> *He is a giraffe.*
> *Jessica's desk is a garbage pail.*

In the memoir section in Chapter 4, we provide a detailed description of strategies to work with metaphors and similes within a unit of study.

CONCLUSION

One of the biggest challenges for teachers is triggering background knowledge and developing the vocabulary that is necessary for students to comprehend the content they are expected to learn. In this chapter, we have provided an array of activities to connect the new concepts that we want the students to know with the knowledge that they already have. This process is key to developing meaningful learning experiences for EL students. We have emphasized the connection between background knowledge and vocabulary, providing specific strategies that connect new words with words students already have in their repertoire. We have also discussed morphology and syntactic structures that are particularly challenging for EL and struggling students. Finally, we have focused on figurative language structures that can be difficult to understand for upper elementary second language learners, and we have presented examples of how classroom teachers have confronted those challenges.

QUESTIONS FOR REFLECTION

Try to answer as many questions as you can:

1. Think about a new experience that you have had and the new vocabulary related to a learning experience (i.e., learning how to swim, ski, horseback ride, etc.). What new words specifically related to this experience did you learn? How did the context support your new learning and long-term memory of the words?

2. Observe a couple of classrooms where teachers approach the teaching of vocabulary differently. For example, observe a classroom where drills and memorization are used for vocabulary teaching, and spend time in another classroom where the focus is on word association and teaching new words in context. Which strategy works better?

3. Try to exercise your knowledge of Tier 1 and Tier 2 words. Can you find a Tier 2 equivalent for the word *angry*? Can you find a Tier 1 equivalent for the word *conscious*?

2

From Social to Academic Language

A Curriculum of Talk

One recurring theme in our conversations with teachers of EL and struggling students is the need to develop academic language across all curriculum areas and through the interactions that occur in school. In our conversations with teachers, they consistently refer to the difficulty that their students have when they try to participate in conversations within academic contexts. During a recent discussion we had with Grace and Karen, a team of fifth-grade dual language teachers, they expressed their concern this way: *"Our children have a very hard time telling us what they know. They just don't have the language to even ask the questions that would clarify what they don't understand."* Peter, a third-grade teacher of a monolingual classroom where 40% of the students are ELs and the rest struggling learners, said something similar: *"We need to give them [the children] words they can use to discuss the things that come up as we delve into the curriculum. I am deeply concerned about oral and written responses and critical thinking skills. With our population of students, we need to create spaces where they have meaningful discussions with each other, and we as teachers need to use sophisticated words and language when we talk to them."*

very interesting

DEVELOPING ORAL LANGUAGE

There has been an important body of research about the need to establish a curriculum of talk in the classroom, as a key element in the process of learning (Calkins, 2001; Church, Baskwill, & Swain, 2007, Gibbons, 2006; Hudelson, 1994). These writers and many others suggest that "talk is a major means by which learners explore the relationship between what they already know and new observations or interpretations which they meet" (Cullinan, 1993, p. 2). Lucy Calkins (2001) writes in *The Art of Teaching Reading*,

> In schools, talk is sometimes valued and sometimes avoided, but—and this is surprising—talk is rarely taught. It is rare to hear teachers discuss their efforts to teach students to talk well. Yet talk, like reading and writing, is a major motor—I could even say the major motor—of intellectual development. (p. 226)

Unfortunately, despite the teachers' concerns, we have both observed that in most classrooms we visit there is very little talk; and when teachers make an effort to have collaborative discussions, they control every interaction strictly through direct directions and questions. In the best of circumstances, when teachers make conscious efforts to facilitate conversations, the dialogue is contrived and stilted. The students don't build on each other's comments even when the teachers attempt to guide the discussions through language prompts or sentence starters.

In this chapter, we focus on the development of oral language and listening comprehension. These skills establish the foundation for the development of language as well as literacy. Our main concern is to lay out a plan for how teachers could organize a curriculum of talk in the classroom that reaches across all curriculum areas. In addition, we want to describe strategies for supporting the teaching and learning of academic discourse. We want teachers to plan as deliberately for students to listen and speak as they plan for reading and writing throughout the school day. Production of language will not take place unless children have an opportunity to listen, understand, and begin to experiment with language in order to communicate. It is essential for second language learners that they have multiple opportunities to experiment with language by speaking and listening in deliberate dialogues throughout the school day.

THE SOCIAL AND ACADEMIC LANGUAGE CONTINUUM

When we think about creating spaces where students can practice talking and listening within an academic setting, we need to establish the difference between social and academic language in order to move the children along the language continuum. Although we tend to think about academic and social language as two separate realms, in reality they form part of a language learning process where the context and the topic play a major role. Social language is the kind of language that we use in everyday communication doing routine activities, talking to friends and family, talking on the telephone, or sending e-mails to friends. These interactions require that both speaker and listener be communicating about the same thing and that the listener and speaker respond to each other; it is the language of social exchange.

Children develop social language naturally as they speak to their friends and family. EL students develop this type of English language quickly because children are social creatures, and they want to interact with their English-speaking peers—they naturally want to communicate with other children, to participate in conversations, to share their thoughts. If children have developed social language in their native language, they transfer these skills as they learn their second language vocabulary. Examples of social language would be:

- Give me the ball.
- Yesterday I went to the park with my mother.
- Can I have a drink of water?

All these situations refer to events within the child's realm of experience, to the here and now.

To master academic subjects in school, students need to learn academic language, which Cummins describes as knowledge of the oral and written registers of school (Cummins, 1979, 2000). In other words, you need academic language in order to understand and describe the concepts you are learning. Academic language is therefore associated with higher order thinking skills such as describing, explaining, comparing and contrasting, inferring, or evaluating information. It entails knowledge of abstract vocabulary and the ability to describe situations without contextual clues.

In the following conversation, we can see an example of a child who does not have this capacity yet:

Student   The fire. It started there, and we had to run. The window was closed and . . .

Teacher   Where did the fire start?

Student   Ah! over there . . . in the kitchen. The window was closed and we couldn't open it.

Teacher   Who was with you?

Student   My mother . . . and then, the window was closed and he was in the street.

Teacher   Who was in the street?

Student   My father.

In this interaction, the student does not take into account the fact that the teacher was not present when the fire took place. He does not understand that they don't share the same background knowledge. His recounting of his experience lacks precision; he is telling the story as if the teacher had been present. The conversation and the language used would have been different if the child had described the situation taking into account that the listener was not with him during the fire:

Student   Yesterday, we had a fire in my house. The kitchen, where the fire started, had a window, but it was stuck and we could not open it. My mother and I ran to the street where my father was waiting.

In this recounting of the same event, we notice that the vocabulary is more precise and that the sentences are more sophisticated and provide more information. The story is clear. The speaker has taken into account that the listener was not present and through his language creates a vivid image. Presenting the information in such a way requires that the student has opportunities to practice and that the teacher scaffolds the conversations so that they become more detailed and take into account what the listener does and doesn't know. We can model using this kind of language in the classroom, being explicit and precise when we communicate with the children.

To promote the development of oral academic language in our classrooms, we need to foster conversations and discussions about what the students are reading, thinking, and learning. The connections that students make between what they know, what other students around them know, and what the text says form the basis for developing academic language.

In the language continuum at one end, we have social contextualized language, which is deeply supported by the context. Meaning is negotiated between the speaker and the listener. At the opposite end, we have written academic language, which can be abstract (meaning there is no contextual support) and which relies completely on words to convey meaning. In the middle of this continuum, we find different levels on which social and academic language interact. Figure 2.1 illustrates the social to academic language continuum.

Figure 2.1 The Social and Academic Language Continuum

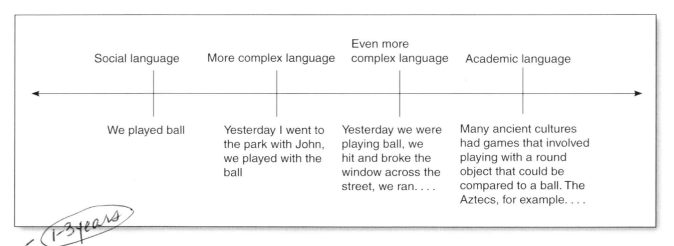

Social and academic language can be learned simultaneously. Social language, or BICS (Basic Interpersonal Communicative Skills; Cummins, Baker, & Hornberger, 2001), can be developed in 1 to 3 years. Mastering social language is not a prerequisite to learning academic language. It takes a long time for EL and struggling students to develop the kind of language that they need in order to be successful in school, the language that Cazden (1992) calls the "discourse of school" and that Cummins refers to as CALP (Cognitive Academic Language Proficiency; Cummins, 1985). The development of academic language is a long process that can take 7 years even in the best of circumstances (Baker, 2006; Collier, 1995; Cummins, 1979; Fillmore & Snow, 2000; Snow et al., 2005).

Many teachers assume that when children have social language they are ready to succeed in school, but that is not so. It is natural to assume that conversational fluency extends to all areas of language, but in fact, conversational ability is only a small portion of the language skills needed to be successful in school (Collier, 1995). Although many EL and struggling learners may do well in school in the primary grades, where language use is more concrete and teaching relies more on visuals, audiovisuals, and hands-on experiences, they fall behind when confronted with the requirements of the curriculum in the upper grades, which requires deeper knowledge of the language. By the time they enter middle school, children cannot be successful without a good command of academic language and without an extensive vocabulary (Collier, 1995; Snow et al., 2005).

WHAT IS A CURRICULUM OF TALK?

When we talk to teachers about the importance of developing listening and speaking skills in their students, they tell us about the pressure they feel as they strive to cover all the areas of the curriculum within the limited hours of school; within this context, listening and speaking do not seem as important as reading and writing. In our discussions, we try to stress the fact that listening and speaking skills establish the foundation for the development of academic language and are essential for the development of reading and writing skills.

The whole purpose of conversation is to understand what other people think and to share our thinking. It is through talk that a great part of our learning occurs. During classroom conversations, children have opportunities to exchange their points of view with other children; they experiment with ways of expressing themselves; they hear and incorporate *(handwritten: why talk is important)* new ideas; and they listen to more sophisticated ways of expression, which they understand through contextual clues and eventually mimic (Gibbons, 2006).

Planning for a curriculum of talk means that we plan the curricular units we will teach, and we set up situations where students will be able to talk about their learning experiences. Classroom talk can take many forms: We can set up a time when students report on what they have learned; we can organize student-led discussions around a specific topic; we can start a cycle of storytelling; or we can have whole-class discussions and turn and talk times during read aloud. The important thing is that we create the conditions where students speak and listen to each other's ideas. We do not leave language development to chance, but we plan different kinds of conversations in different areas of the curriculum. *(handwritten margin: ✭ Strategies)*

Table 2.2 shows an example of Peter's plan to incorporate different types of oral interactions in his class, across the different units of study that he was working with in the course of a month. Notice how he has incorporated conversations in all areas, including math.

Table 2.2   Mr. Richards's Plan for Oral Language

Writing Memoir	**Reading** Nonfiction Biographies	**Social Studies** World Communities	**Science** Plant and Animal Adaptations	**Math** Fractions
• Turn and talk during read aloud • Whole-class conversations • Storytelling • Fishbowl conversations	• Interactive read aloud discussions • Turn and talk • Partner talk • Book clubs	• Collaborative group work: Report on group projects • Group discussions during read aloud/ shared reading/ shared writing	• Collaborative group work and class presentations of different projects • Presentation of our projects to other third-grade classrooms	• Collaborative group work to discuss word problems

GOALS OF A CURRICULUM OF TALK: THE ROLE OF CONVERSATION

Maintaining Focus

At the beginning of the school year, it is important to get children to practice listening and then responding, challenging them to remain focused on the topics discussed as classroom conversations evolve. The first step in this process is to make children aware of how a literate conversation works. Delpit (2006) reminds teachers that they need to be very explicit about the structure of literate conversations as well as the culture of schools, so that children can understand the discourse and the expectations that schools carry. This is very important for ELs and other struggling learners, because many children come from cultures where they are not involved in conversations, and they are expected to sit passively while adults speak, so they have not been exposed to the kind of protocol that literate discussions require.

Understanding How Literate Conversations Function

We want children to become metacognitive of the structure of good conversations by setting up ground rules that they come to understand in time. Spending some time setting up the protocol of conversations creates an environment that leads to literate discussions later on.

Many teachers we know spend time explicitly teaching and modeling the structure of literate conversations for children. Table 2.3 is an example of a chart we saw in a classroom.

Table 2.3 Conversation Chart

How do we have a good conversation?

- We listen to each other before we think of our answer.
- We try to add on, basing our input on what we have listened to.
- We ask others to repeat if we don't understand something.
- We pause to think and to process the information before we speak.
- We ask for examples when we don't understand.

Peter and one of his colleagues decided to bring their two third-grade classrooms together to model for their students how a good conversation works. They asked the children to take notes about the conversational moves they saw. Fifty children watched the teachers as they discussed a book, using language prompts and waiting patiently for their time to speak. They each gave their opinions about the characters using language prompts, read small passages from the book to support or reject their initial ideas, and clarified and expanded concepts for each other. After they modeled the conversation, they gave each group of students an opportunity to have a book talk, referring to the notes they had taken when they observed the conversation. Subsequently, Peter noticed that the children tried to imitate the moves they had seen during the teachers' conversation.

Understanding and Assessing the Qualities of a Good Speaker

We need to be able to assess the progress of our students' conversational skills as we assess their progress in other areas.

Peter and a group of his colleagues developed some clear goals for what they wanted their students to achieve in terms of conversational skills. They used the New York State English Language Arts (ELA) Standards as a guide for their discussions. They started with the following questions:

- What are the skills that the students need in order to have good conversational skills?
- How do we assess the progress of the students so that we can help them improve?

Here is a list of the goals that they decided they wanted to work on:

- Students will be able to begin conversations on their own around the topics they are studying without the teacher being the initiator.
- Students will integrate new vocabulary and language structures in their conversations as they talk to each other.

- Students will develop the ability to stay on topic during class discussions.
- Students will be able to summarize information, focusing on the main idea and providing a few supporting details.
- Students will take into account the listeners as they relate information.
- Students will understand that conversation involves turn taking.

To support their goals and assess their students' progress, they created the Conversation Assessment Form (Table 2.4). For a full-sized printable version of the Conversation Assessment Form, see http://www.corwin.com/connectingcontent4ell.

Table 2.4   Conversation Assessment Form

Qualities of Good Speaking During a Conversation						
Name of Student	Begins conversations	Uses new words/ language structures	Maintains focus in conversation	Summarizes (main idea with supporting details)	Takes into account the listener when speaking	Understands turn taking

Key

1: student owns the skill   2: student is approximating   Blank: no evidence

Copyright © 2011 by Corwin. All rights reserved. Reprinted from *Connecting Content and Academic Language for English Learners and Struggling Students, Grades 2–6*, by Ruth Swinney and Patricia Velasco. Thousand Oaks, CA: Corwin, www.corwin.com. Reproduction authorized only for the local school site or nonprofit organization that has purchased this book.

Spending Time Focusing on Listening Skills

Assessing oral language skills is easier than assessing listening skills, but how do we measure progress in listening skills? Pauline Gibbons observes that the teaching of listening is often overlooked, when we group together speaking and listening skills under one umbrella. We tend to focus more on the speaking part, yet the development of listening skills is a key component for language development (Gibbons, 1991, 2006).

Just as oral language can be seen as a continuum, there are different types or levels of listening comprehension. The most common form is explicit comprehension. In this example, the listener merely understands what is explicitly stated in the phrase, "Yesterday, I had a fight with my sister." The listener may not draw any inferences or conclusions, nor elaborate on what is being said, but the listener understands what is specifically stated. At the other end, there are high levels of comprehension in which the listener can make inferences, visualize, predict, or establish conclusions.

For language to work, it is assumed that both the speaker and the listener are cooperating and interested in their communication. The speaker is attempting to convey only the information that is relevant or interesting for the listener. The listener is trying to ascertain the importance and relevance of what the speaker is trying to convey. The speaker will adjust his or her speech, explanations, and length of description according to the reactions he or she sees from the listener.

The development of listening skills starts by helping students develop a context for what the conversation is going to be about. This is what is called "pre-listening," or "targeting listening," in which we help our students prepare for the information that is coming. For example, if we are going to have a conversation about proper behavior in the cafeteria, we may start by framing the subject of our discussion: "We are going to talk about our behavior in the cafeteria." If we are having a conversation about character motivation following a read aloud, we may say, "We are going to talk about the friendship between Poppleton and Cherry Sue." We are letting children know the subject of the conversation, so that they prepare.

We also want to be specific in showing students what they should be doing during listening. Table 2.5 provides an example of a chart we saw in a classroom.

Table 2.5   Sample Listening Chart

Ways in which we listen during a conversation:
• We look at the person who is speaking and think about what the person is saying, trying to make sense of it.
• Then, we decide if we want to respond, either by adding more information, or by asking for clarification or more examples.

Peter and his colleagues felt that developing an assessment tool for their students' conversational skills was very helpful in formulating a plan to get children to meet the goals that they had developed. They decided that they wanted to follow the same process in order to improve the listening skills of their students.

They started by asking some essential questions, after checking the New York State ELA Standards for listening:

- What makes a good listener?
- What are the skills that the students need to have in order to have good listening skills?
- How do we assess the progress of the students so that we can help them improve?

After much discussion, they decided that they had to work on some very specific goals:

- The student listens carefully so that he can respond appropriately to what he has heard.
- The student connects the information she is receiving with her prior knowledge.
- The student responds to others by asking questions that are relevant.
- The student follows instructions.
- The student distinguishes between fact and opinion.
- The student focuses on the person who is speaking.
- The student can take notes as the teacher is reading aloud or explaining a concept.

The teachers then put those goals in a chart (see Table 2.6) to assess their students' progress in listening skills. For a full-sized printable version of the Listening Assessment Form, see http://www.corwin.com/connectingcontent4ell.

Table 2.6 Listening Assessment Form

	Qualities of Good Listening					
Name of Student	Responds appropriately to what is heard	Connects new information with prior experience	Responds to others by asking relevant questions	Follows instructions	Distinguishes between fact and opinion	Can take notes as teacher speaks or reads

Key

1: student owns the skill   2: student is approximating   Blank: no evidence

Copyright © 2011 by Corwin. All rights reserved. Reprinted from *Connecting Content and Academic Language for English Learners and Struggling Students, Grades 2–6*, by Ruth Swinney and Patricia Velasco. Thousand Oaks, CA: Corwin, www.corwin.com. Reproduction authorized only for the local school site or nonprofit organization that has purchased this book.

Strategies to Develop Speaking and Listening Comprehension

 Partnerships provide great opportunities for students to practice their listening and speaking skills. Many teachers establish partnerships for conversations during read aloud, and those partnerships remain stable for a period of time so that children can work together and exchange ideas. When there are new EL arrivals in the classroom, the teachers set up triads, in which a bilingual child negotiates meaning for the new arrival, and an English-speaking child is the third partner in this group. In this way, all children are engaged in the conversation.

Peter has a chart in his class (Table 2.7) delineating clearly his expectations for his students during partner talk.

Table 2.7 Partner Talk Chart

Expectations during partner talk:

- We look at our partner and listen carefully.
- We patiently wait our turn to share our ideas.
- We sit straight and turn our heads as we start our conversation.

During a class conversation, the teacher often stops and asks children to turn to their partners and tell them what they have heard so that children can interpret and summarize what has been said. He also has listening skills prompts, which give children the language to ask for clarification when they don't understand something (see Table 2.8).

Table 2.8 Chart of Listening Skills Prompts

What we can say when we don't understand:

- Can you repeat, please?
- Can you say that again?
- Could you expand on that, please?
- I did not understand what you said.

---

check for understanding

In the course of a conversation, he often stops and asks children if there are things they don't understand before he continues a discussion.

The teacher often tells children what conversational moves he wants them to work on during their partner talk. For example, one day he said to the students, *"Today, I want to spend time observing how you start your conversations and how you respond to your partner's comments."* Another time, he told the children that before accountable talk he was going to observe how they incorporated into their discussion the new language prompts he had modeled and posted. In this way, he carefully guided the children to integrate the new conversational skills into their repertoire.

DIFFERENT TYPES OF CLASSROOM CONVERSATIONS THAT SUPPORT LISTENING AND SPEAKING IN THE CLASSROOM

When we walk into classrooms that are silent for extended periods, and the only voice is that of the teacher, we feel that the students are missing a key learning experience. In contrast, when we walk into a classroom where there is a healthy buzz, where students are engaged in talking to partners about their work or in whole-classroom conversations or doing collaborative work with peers, we see students in the process of making meaning. The more the children talk about their learning, the more they will be able to integrate new language and concepts into their repertoire and take responsibility for their learning.

When we refer to classroom talk, we mean all the different interactions that a teacher may structure around learning during literacy work, in the content areas, or in social situations. The challenge for teachers is to set up structures in which children increasingly take more responsibility in initiating and carrying on the different types of conversations that will happen in the classroom.

At the beginning of this process, the teacher is the facilitator of the conversations, and after the children speak, she may ask students to turn and talk to their partners to give their opinions. In a general discussion, she may ask children to add to the discussion, to agree or disagree; or she may ask a particular child to speak. The teacher may coach individual EL children to respond, asking them to rehearse their answers before speaking. She often reminds students to look at each other as they speak, rather than looking at her.

As students get used to having classroom conversations, the teacher's role as facilitator diminishes; eventually, students speak when they hear something they can add on to, or when they disagree.

Conversations in the classroom can take many forms. Following are descriptions of five of them, with a summary in Table 2.9.

Class meetings may be part of the morning meetings as children are asked to bring newspaper clippings of a story of interest. Sometimes the discussions may focus on particular issues confronting the classroom, such as lunchroom fights and bullying. In this type of conversation, children sit in the meeting place facing the teacher.

Accountable Talk™ (Resnick, 1999; Wolf, Crosson, & Resnick, 2006) provides teachers with guidelines to help them facilitate focused discussions around academic topics. During these conversations, the class discusses a book or a topic. As students develop the tools to remain focused on the topic discussed, they learn to carry the discussion with minimal facilitation from the teacher. Accountable Talk involves three dimensions: accountability to the learning community, in which participants listen to and build their contributions in response to those of others; accountability to accepted standards of reasoning, where talk is connected to the subject being discussed and makes sense; and talk that is based explicitly on facts or the texts being discussed (Michaels, O'Connor, & Resnick, 2007). During Accountable Talk, students are taught to speak to the topic, offer evidence for their assertions, and listen and respond to each other. During interactive read aloud, the teachers may have Accountable Talk once or twice a week, involving the whole class. This does not preclude Accountable Talk around other topics at other times. In this type of conversation, children are seated in a circle so that they can see each other as they speak, rather than facing the teacher, and they take turns talking to each other. The teacher acts as a facilitator and eventually relinquishes responsibility for facilitating to the children. You can see an example of Accountable Talk in Chapter 4.

For additional information about Accountable Talk, see http://ifl.lrdc.pitt.edu/ifl/index .php/home/.

For *partner talk*, children are in two- or three-way partnerships for independent reading for focused class discussions and for interactive talk during read aloud. During turn and talk, they are prompted to turn to their partner and talk for specific purposes. Children are asked to refer to conversational prompts (a repertoire of responses that children can use in the conversation) in order to pose their ideas and ask others about their ideas.

Small-group collaborative work involves a group of students working together on a particular topic, for example, clarifying how to solve a math problem, presenting a joint book report, or working on a science experiment. Collaborative work can also take the form of researching and developing a project that can be presented to the whole class.

Small-group collaborative work allows students to hear a wider range of language and have more language directed to them than is possible in a whole-class context. They have more opportunities to interact and take turns. If the teacher is not around, the student can take risks and ask questions that clarify concepts. Small-group collaborative work can provide an environment in which less confident students feel more comfortable to talk.

Fishbowl conversations consist of two concentric circles of students, a small circle within a larger one. The inner circle holds a conversation about a book or about a particular topic, while the outer circle takes notes about the characteristics of the conversation, for example, how students are using language prompts, how they are following the classroom rubrics for conversation, or what new concepts that they are learning. Only people in the inner circle are allowed to speak. After the conversation, the children in the outer circle talk about the quality of the conversation. The teacher only gets involved if the conversation loses focus. This is a great way to make children metacognitive about the structure of conversations and to help them to take ownership of their conversations. It is also a way to hold children accountable for improving the quality of conversations in the classroom and to help them to develop listening and note-taking skills.

Table 2.9   Types of Classroom Conversations

Types of Classroom Conversations	Structure
Class meetings	Children sit together in the meeting place facing the teacher.
Whole-class conversations using Accountable Talk (Institute for Learning)	Discussions after read aloud. Children form a circle where they can see each other as they talk.
Partner talk	Children are in two- or three-way partnerships for independent reading and for interactive talk during read aloud.
Small-group collaborative work	Students work together on a joint project and develop a plan for reporting on their work.
Fishbowl conversations	A group of students sit in an inner circle holding a conversation, while another group sits in an outer circle observing the conversational moves. After the conversation, the outer circle students report on their observations.

Listening and speaking provide the basis for having a good conversation in which the speaker and the listener alternate their roles; they build on each other's comments and make an explicit effort to understand each other. These skills can be modeled, reinforced by the use of charts, and practiced in the classroom. These focused conversations will not be perfect, but practicing and monitoring by the students and teacher will greatly contribute to the learning of oral academic discourse. In the following section, we discuss the importance of questions and their relationship to higher order thinking skills.

Deepening the Level of Our Conversations Through Our Questions

Hall and Walsh (2002) write that the three-part sequence of teacher initiation, student response, and teacher evaluation (IRE) is the most common pattern of second language classroom discourse and that the teacher usually initiates the interaction using direct questions. We often observe teachers asking students questions that require only direct answers, such as, "Were Poppleton and Cherry Sue friends or enemies?" This kind of questioning has only one right answer, and it does not require that students think and evaluate before answering. This kind of interaction sets the teacher as a judge and evaluator and is not conducive to real classroom conversations where students listen to each other and have an exchange of opinions. In contrast, we can use our questions to get students to think about different possible answers to the questions we pose and to search their experience and knowledge for a reasonable answer. The previous question could be better structured as follows: "What can we say about the relationship between Poppleton and Cherry Sue?"

In the following example, Rachel Bard is guiding her fourth-grade students to dig deeper into the text by asking thoughtful questions.

Rachel	I have observed that when you do your KWL charts in your notebooks you do not ask questions about things you don't know. For example, one question I saw was, "What is slavery?" All of you know what slavery is, so that is not a question that would make you understand the text deeper. Today we are going to ask questions that will help us understand more profoundly, this means better, the text about slavery in New York State that we are reading.

She writes on chart paper, "How can we ask a thinking question about this text?"

Arancis	I have two examples about how to make a strong solid question. First, ask a question that makes you do research to find the answer. You don't know the answer. Second, ask a question based on the text that you don't understand.
Franklyn	When you read a text you stop and think: What is this trying to say?
Vanessa	You can ask a good question by looking at titles and subtitles.
Rachel	All those ideas are just great, think about what you just said and let's read the text to see the kinds of thoughtful questions we may ask.

She reads aloud a passage from the textbook titled *The New York State Story* (Sesso & Weller, 2000). After reading the passage, she posts a chart with a list of sample questions. These are "who," "what," "why," "how" questions:

- How did New Yorkers fight slavery?
- How were the Africans being treated?

- Were there slaves in New York State?
- Where is New York State?
- What was the life of the slaves like?
- Why did New Yorkers have slaves?

She then asks children to evaluate the questions by turning to the child next to them to discuss their answers. She moves around the group to listen to the partner conversations.

Darlene	I think that "How were the Africans being treated?" is a weak question because we already know how they were being treated.
Roberto (her partner)	I disagree because if you know how they were being treated you get an idea about their life. I think that the weak question is "Were there slaves in New York State?" because the text is about slaves in New York.
Johana	I think that asking "Where was New York State?" is a bad . . . I mean weak question because that is not in the text.
Arancis (her partner)	I agree because people already know this. Why ask the question?

The discussion continues. Then, Rachel reads the text again and asks children to work with their talking partners to formulate thoughtful questions that they can add to their KWL charts.

In this example, we see that Rachel set up a situation where her children had the opportunity to talk in small and large groups and to interact with their peers through collaborative partner work. She encouraged her students to be thoughtful when they work on their KWL charts by asking open-ended questions that helped them to delve deeper into the text, rather than direct questions about the text that only require one answer.

Setting the Stage for Academic Language Development

Lee and VanPatten (2003) see the teacher as the architect who carefully designs talk in his classroom to help the development of academic language. The teacher creates situations in which he asks deliberate questions, carefully selects participants for the discussions, and ensures that the conversation is meaningful.

Making classroom talk meaningful requires careful planning. The teacher needs to scaffold the conversations by setting up a series of strategies to help students to develop precision and elaboration in their discussions.

Modeling Sophisticated Language

We often hear teachers simplifying language in order to be understood. For example, we observed a teacher say the following to a group of second graders: "Go out this way." We asked her what may be a more explicit way to say that simple sentence in order to stretch the language of the children. She replied, "Well, I could say: 'Please use this exit.'" Later on, we observed the same teacher ask the children to "separate the unifix cubes by color." A more academic way of conveying the same meaning would have been to use Tier 2 words (see Chapter 1) such as *classify* or *sort* instead of *separate*. We must not only make language comprehensible but also help kids to find new ways of expressing ideas in an academic school context.

Modeling sophisticated language also means stretching the language. This means modeling many words and many forms of expression and giving students alternative words in order to enrich their vocabulary. Figure 2.10 is a synonym chart that Grace posted, after telling her students that she was very "bored" by their repetitive use of *said*.

Using Language Prompts

Language prompts are sentence starters that reflect particular thinking skills; these help students use higher order thinking skills during whole-class and small-group discussions. They function as temporary scaffolds to provide the language that children can use to express their thinking and to support each other's ideas. For example, they can agree or disagree with each other, they can ask for an expansion of an idea, or they can compare and contrast. Below are some examples of language prompts:

- I agree with what you said because. . . .
- Could you repeat what you are saying?
- My prediction is that . . . will happen, because. . . .
- I wonder if. . . .
- Another example of that is. . . . .

| **Figure 2.10** | Example Synonym Chart |

From Grace Stevenson.

Language prompts are often posted around the meeting area, and they change as students integrate them into their repertoire.

Figure 2.11 shows a chart that Grace uses to help her fifth-grade students to focus on the conversational prompts during partner talk. Here, they are practicing clarification. Notice that she posts a date (10/20) to make sure these conversational prompts are temporary scaffolds.

Amplifying (or Elaborating)

The language that the teacher uses in the classroom is a key element in promoting language comprehension and acquisition (Gibbons, 1991; Long, 2007). When we use comprehensible language side by side with more elaborate language, we give our students an opportunity to understand what we are saying, as well as the chance to hear more sophisticated forms of saying the same thing. We have to be very conscious during classroom conversations to move the children toward more sophisticated language rather than accepting

Figure 2.11   Accountable Talk: Practicing Clarification Chart

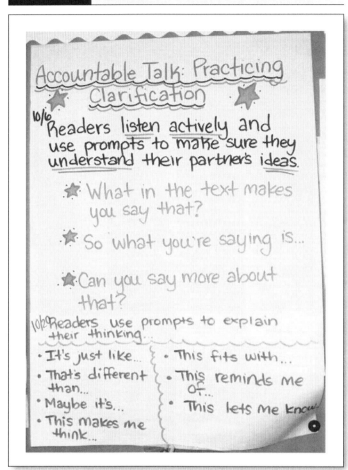

From Grace Stevenson.

simple answers. At the same time, conversations have to be more supportive rather than directive (Long, 2007).

Asking Precise Questions

Teachers should be relentless in demanding good and precise answers, but this only happens if we ask precise questions. If we ask, *"Did you like Precious and the Boo Hag?"* the student will probably say, *"Yes"* or *"No."* If we ask, *"What was your favorite part in the book?"* we will very likely get a more substantial answer.

Recasting

Recasting is a way of reformulating, correcting, or giving the appropriate language structure or vocabulary to our students (Ellis & Fotos, 1999). It means that the teacher will repeat using the correct word or syntactic structure, emphasizing through intonation or repetition what needs to be corrected. Recasting allows students to receive immediate feedback, and it has proven far more successful than saying, "You made a mistake; this is the way that you have to say it."

In Table 2.12, notice how the teacher deliberately builds on all these strategies for practicing and strengthening the academic language development of her students, by supporting them in building an argument.

Table 2.12   Conversation Example

After reading aloud "Colonial Life" by Brendan January, the teacher pointed to a picture of the Pilgrims in Massachusetts and said:	
Teacher	Let's think about what we learned today. What made the Pilgrims take such a difficult trip?
Roberto	To be free.
Teacher	To be free to do what? **(PRECISE QUESTION)**
Luz	They wanted to . . .
Roberto	To pay.
Teacher	To pray. **(RECASTING)**
Teacher	Couldn't they pray in England, where they were born?

Maria	They were afraid . . .
Luz	They were attacked.
Teacher	Why were they attacked? You mean they were persecuted? That means they were mistreated. **(AMPLIFYING)**
Roberto	Religion.
Teacher	What do you want to say about religion? **(PRECISE QUESTION)**
Luz	They wanted . . . to . . .
Maria	To practice . . .
Teacher	They wanted to practice? That does not make sense. Explain.
Maria	They wanted to be free to practice.
Teacher	To practice what? **(PRECISE QUESTION)**
Maria	To practice religion!
Teacher	Who wanted religious freedom?
All the students	The Pilgrims!
Teacher	Where did the Pilgrims go to find religious freedom?
Roberto	America.
Teacher	Let's put it all together. **(BUILDING AN ARGUMENT)**
All the students	Pilgrims came to America to find religious freedom.
Teacher	That is right. The Pilgrims came to America in order to be able to practice their religion freely. Let's all say it. (Teacher writes the sentence on chart paper)
Group repeats	The Pilgrims came to America in order to practice their religion freely.
Teacher	Now, we are going to tell Ms. Jackson (art teacher) what you just learned.
Roberto to Ms. Jackson	The Pilgrims came to America because in England they were not free to practice their religion. They thought that in America they would be able to practice their religion.

Notice that the conversation begins with a question ("What made the Pilgrims take such a difficult trip?") and ends with the group having worked towards a more sophisticated explanation with different kinds of scaffolding. These conversations do not require much time, but they do require awareness on the part of the teacher.

Storytelling

Storytelling is an activity that helps students develop speaking and listening skills and encourages them to communicate their thoughts and feelings to their audience. When you create a story or tell about an experience that you had, there are many elements that the

*[handwritten margin note: Elements Associated with Academic Lang:
• Precision
• Explicitness
• Orientation → Speaker]*

speaker or storyteller has to take into account: details about the setting, the characters that propel the story, the problems or challenges that are faced, and the resolution or end of the story. The sequence of events is important, and words such as *before* and *after*, or cause-and-effect conjunctions such as *because* or *however*, become important in the success of this activity. Storytelling requires elements that are associated with academic language: precision, explicitness, and orientation towards the speaker.

One way to initiate storytelling is by starting with a shared experience that the class has had, such as a class trip or a fight during gym, and then give children the opportunity to tell it and embellish it from their perspective.

As you start a cycle of storytelling, children can be encouraged to talk with their families about stories that they share, and you can set aside a part of the day for storytelling. You can also ask children to take a story you have read and change the setting or the ending to fit their imaginations. Later on in the "Memoir" chapter (Chapter 4), we give concrete examples of how storytelling can work within a unit of study.

CONCLUSION

[handwritten margin note: Bridge → Social / academic]

Focused classroom conversation in all its manifestations is the bridge that links social and academic language (Gibbons, 1991). In this chapter, we have argued for the need to think about the development of oral language in all subject areas. When we set up situations in which children can talk about their learning, we are helping them to organize their thoughts and synthesize the information that they are receiving. In addition, they are expanding their language repertoire. The teacher plays a crucial role in this process. Her presence is necessary for modeling language, for supporting her students' conversations, and for organizing a curriculum of talk that covers all subject areas and uses different interactions in the classroom.

QUESTIONS FOR REFLECTION

Try to answer as many questions as you can:

1. As you plan a unit in social studies or science, can you design a schedule for several classroom conversations that will provide opportunities for students to talk to each other about their learning experiences? Could you list the objectives for each conversation?

2. Visit two different classrooms during class conversations. Observe the conversational moves of each teacher as well as the flow of conversation of the students. How much does each teacher control the discussion? Is there a clear goal for each conversation? Do the discussions enrich the language and knowledge of the students? How would you plan the conversations differently?

3. Could you provide your own examples of amplifying, using precise questions, and recasting? Try to use these three strategies in your next class conversation to support your students in developing an argument.

3

Structures of Balanced Literacy That Support English Language Learners and Struggling Students

WHAT IS BALANCED LITERACY?

Balanced literacy is a framework for teaching reading and writing that provides students a consistent and coherent plan for the development of language and literacy (Calkins, 2001, Chen & Mora-Flores, 2006). Language development is embedded in the structures of balanced literacy: Listening and speaking skills are deep-rooted throughout the different components, as there is constant interaction between students through whole-class and small-group instruction, partner talk, and collaborative work. There is a high level of engagement, as children are expected to be involved in their learning by participating in a mini-lesson, reading and writing independently, discussing their work with partners, or sharing their work with the whole class. The writing work is built around the lives of the children, as they select topics that reflect their experiences, while at the same time they expand their language skills. There is also ongoing interaction with teachers as they use an array of strategies to model for students how reading and writing work. Teachers implementing this framework use an integrated approach that provides students many opportunities on a daily basis to practice reading and writing at their own level of proximal development (Vygotsky & Cole, 1978), with the teacher modeling, supporting, and finally guiding them towards independent work.

The main components of balanced literacy are:

- Interactive Read Aloud
- Shared Reading
- Guided Reading
- Independent Reading
- Shared Writing
- Interactive Writing
- Independent Writing

During ***Interactive Read Aloud***, the teacher reads to the whole class or to a small group of students, exposing them to a variety of literary genres. As the teacher reads, he is modeling an array of reading comprehension strategies such as getting the main idea, inferring, visualizing, questioning, or predicting. As he reads aloud, the teacher may ask students to turn to their partners at different points of the reading, to talk about different aspect of the book that he may find important for understanding the text, or to help students develop critical thinking skills. The teacher uses strategies to push the thinking of the students, such as ***think alouds*** and ***turn and talk***. Once or twice a week, he may facilitate whole-class conversations where the class discusses different aspects of the text using the structures of Accountable Talk (Wolf, Crosson, & Resnick, 2006).

Shared Reading is an interactive reading experience that gives children the opportunity to observe and participate in a reading activity and allows the teacher to model specific reading strategies. The text may be read several times for different purposes. It is presented in an enlarged format so that children can join the teacher in reading for specific purposes. For example, in the early primary grades, teachers may read songs, poems, or charts, showing children reading behaviors such as moving from left to right, beginning sounds, endings, punctuation, and practicing fluency, among many others. As children move up in the grades, teachers may use shared reading for multiple purposes; for example, they can explicitly demonstrate how to read textbooks when reading nonfiction texts, indicating the importance of titles and subtitles and other characteristics of the genre; they can expose children to sophisticated vocabulary that they cannot read on their own; they can help students understand how an author's style works; and they can use shared reading to teach syntax within the context of a unit of study. These are just a few examples of ways in which shared reading may be used.

During ***Guided Reading***, teachers work together with a small group of students who need help with the same reading strategies. The main purpose of guided reading is to move students to their next reading level. Students in a guided reading group must be reading the books with 90% accuracy, so that they can understand the book and apply the strategies they are being taught. In this way, they will be able to read more difficult texts on their own. The teacher introduces the book briefly to the group and eases the way into a new reading level by pointing out different vocabulary and roadblocks they may encounter. Then she works individually with each student as she listens to them read. During the guided reading session, the teacher may teach the group a new strategy, such as context clues, letter and sound relationships, word structure, or getting the main idea. The teacher observes the students practicing that strategy. Guided reading groups are not static; they are organized according to the specific needs of students so they change as students progress individually.

During ***Independent Reading***, the teacher models a specific reading strategy to the class through a mini-lesson and then gives the students a block of time to practice the strategy as they read independently. Students select books that are on their reading level—just right books (Allington, 2001)—and read for extended periods of time in the classroom, as well as at home. Periodically, the teachers confer with the students to make sure they are reading on an appropriate level and practicing the strategies they have learned. When students do independent reading, they build fluency (Allington, 2001), increase their vocabulary, and enhance their background knowledge. Independent reading helps students develop the tools to become lifelong readers.

Shared Writing is a balanced literacy component in which the teacher and students collaborate to write a text together on large chart paper or on the board. The text can be a shared experience the class had, such as a class trip, or it can be an original story they are writing together. The teacher writes down what she and the class decide collectively, and in the process she shows the students how to construct the different ideas in terms of vocabulary and sentence structure choices. The teacher has the responsibility for writing the text and using correct spelling and grammar. During this activity, the teacher demonstrates how writing works by showing how ideas are put down on paper and how language structures work.

Interactive Writing is a structure that is used in the early primary grades. Teacher and students share the pen as they write a short text together. Children participate in the writing as they come to the board to write when called by the teacher. During interactive writing, the children become aware of how written language works, as teachers involve them in writing the text. The main purpose of this structure is to show students early strategies and concepts of print (Pinnell & Fountas, 2007).

During ***Independent Writing***, the teacher models a particular strategy to the whole class through a mini-lesson, helping them to grow in their writing, and then gives the students a block of time to write independently about topics that they have chosen. Students work within specific units of study tailored to meet the curricular needs of the grade; for example, they may do a personal narrative unit one month and a nonfiction unit the next. The teacher confers with the students individually to make sure they are using the strategies she is teaching. Many teachers who practice balanced literacy do it within the structure of the ***Reader's and Writer's Workshop***. The workshop model has a defined structure and set of rituals. The teacher starts by modeling a reading or writing skill through a mini-lesson. Students then go back to their tables to read or write independently, applying the new strategy they have learned. Then, there is a share time at the end of the period, where the students contribute what they have worked on, and the teacher reminds them of the new strategy they have learned.

LITERACY PRACTICES THAT SUPPORT LANGUAGE GROWTH

Although all components of balanced literacy are very important for the academic development of all students, we believe that there are some components that are particularly important for ELs and struggling learners, and we specifically focus on them in this book. Their importance stems from the fact that they scaffold language and comprehension. Read aloud and Accountable Talk, shared reading, and shared writing help children understand how academic language works and give the students opportunities to use language for different purposes under the careful guidance of the teacher. The interactive read aloud with accountable conversation immerses children—even those who are in early stages of language acquisition in the language of literacy. Not only will they take on the language forms found in the texts, they will also mimic other speakers if they have the chance, during accountable talk time, to hear people growing ideas through a discussion. Language prompts, which usually are in charts around the room, provide models for more sophisticated ways to ask questions, to clarify things, to start conversations. Teachers scaffold the read aloud as well as the conversations not only through language prompts but also with think alouds, which help children develop critical thinking skills.

Through shared reading and shared writing, children are able to take in the language structures and rhythms of even very sophisticated literate language that they could not access on their own. These structures help children to understand how reading and writing work and to develop reading and writing strategies they will use as their literacy grows. In addition, they provide opportunities for reinforcing and building on oral language and listening skills. Although these two practices are most commonly used in the early childhood grades, for EL and struggling students they should be used across the grades in middle school and high school. Even although these students may not be able to access their own texts because of their reading skills, many of them have sophisticated ideas but lack the language to express them. It is very important to continue exposing them to higher levels of language and thought. In addition, many students begin to see the relationship between oral and printed language during shared reading and shared writing. These three structures—read aloud, shared reading, and shared writing—are very important in the conceptual and linguistic development of the students we have in mind. They offer the necessary support to understand how language works and to use it in meaningful and challenging ways.

ADAPTING BALANCED LITERACY COMPONENTS

A few years ago we led a study group of third-, fourth-, and fifth-grade teachers who work in a variety of public schools in New York City and its suburbs. The purpose of our study group was to collaborate on ways in which we could tailor the balanced literacy structures they were using to better support struggling as well as EL students.

During our first meeting, Karen expressed the frustration she felt as she tried to teach some of her fifth graders by saying, *"Even although I am making all the right teaching moves, I am really frustrated because I cannot reach some students, they just don't get it. I don't know what else to do: I teach engaging mini-lessons, I work in small groups with my students to meet their individual needs. I do interactive read alouds daily. Yet some of my kids are failing."*

Luisa agreed: *"I feel the same way, many of my children do well, but there is a group of students that simply are not ready to move at the pace we are being asked to move through our units of study in reading and writing and in the other content areas."*

Irma: *"Yes!! They are always one or two steps behind! And while the other children move on, the struggling students stay behind and get even more behind as the time goes by. . . ."*

The group of 15 teachers continued a discussion along these terms, expressing their frustration in working with what they call "hard-to-reach students." In the next series of meetings, as teachers continued their discussion, they finally came to a common understanding. If some of their children were not doing well, they deduced, something was missing in their teaching; the problem did not reside in the children, but in how they were being taught. Even though balanced literacy structures support language development, it was apparent that for some children we needed to add scaffolds and modify our teaching in order to help them develop reading and writing skills as well as content knowledge.

As we began to examine the teaching methods that were being used, we were looking for strategies that we could add to the essential components of read alouds, shared reading, and shared writing that the teachers could try in their own classrooms.

The following are a series of modifications that the group decided would scaffold the learning experience for their struggling and EL students.

INTERACTIVE READ ALOUD   *How to:*

Best Practices for All Students

Best practices are relevant to all students. We describe them here because they are particularly important to EL and struggling learners. An ***Interactive Read Aloud*** requires careful selection not only of the book, but also of the thinking skills that you want to model. For purposes of clarity, we have divided the preparation of the read aloud in three distinct parts: before, during, and after the interactive read aloud.

Before the Read Aloud

Plan the specific objectives of the read aloud and the work you will do within the book as you select the text

Book choice is crucial to the read aloud. The read aloud should support the unit of study that you are developing. In addition, a carefully chosen book used in interactive read aloud can be the instrument that launches a new unit. One teacher said, *"For this particular group of students the read aloud could anchor the units of study we are teaching; we could develop some of the* background knowledge *the students need. The important thing is to plan what we are going to do through the read aloud; are we going to focus on developing background knowledge? Are we going to support particular reading skills? For example, reading nonfiction books as one of the read alouds may help develop background knowledge that the students need in order to understand some of the content areas. If the class is engaged in the study of plant and animal adaptations in science, reading a book about how plants respond to light may develop background knowledge that many students do not have, and, in addition, you may show students how to read* nonfiction, *looking at* titles, subtitles, and captions. *If you are working on* inference skills, *you may read a book that has* strong characters *and the students can learn to infer their traits from what they are reading."*

We need to ensure that the books have rich language, reflect different genres, and support the units of study you are teaching either in literacy or in the content areas.

Become very familiar with the book you are reading and decide beforehand the thinking skills you want to emphasize

Read aloud is much more than reading a book. It implies that you have read the book several times and marked the parts where you want to stop and share your thoughts with the students in order to model reading behaviors and help them develop critical thinking skills.

[Handwritten margin notes:]
Book choice
- support unit of study
- Rich language
- Different genres

Non Fiction strategies
- titles, subtitles, captions

Infering - choose book w/ strong characters

Characterization

SALT
Say Act Look Think

Luisa described how her new thinking affected planning for her third graders:

I am reading Jamaica's Find *by Juanita Havill (Havill & O'Brien, 1986) as part of my unit on character study. We will work on inference skills, I will teach them to use the acronym SALT. It stands for the strategy that we know our characters by what they **S**ay, **A**ct, **L**ook, and **T**hink. This implies making an inference, and I am asking them to use a language prompt that will help my students structure these inferences.*

I noticed that Jamaica's mother said: _____. This means that _____.

I'm also using think alouds to infer character traits, using evidence in the text to support what I'm thinking. This would be something like "I noticed that Jamaica's mother said to return the stuffed dog. This means that she is very honest, and she wants Jamaica to be honest too."

During the Read Aloud

Model reading strategies through thinking skills

The best way to teach comprehension strategies is through read aloud. Model the sort of thinking a good reader is apt to do as he or she reads using "think alouds." When teachers think aloud, they are demonstrating explicitly what good readers do when confronted with a text. Here are some of the strategies you could model during read aloud (based on Keene & Zimmerman, 2007):

Strategies
Comprehension
Predicting
Visualizing
Summarizing
Inferring

- Monitoring for comprehension:

  What is going on?

  What is the main issue?

  Why do I think that?
- Predicting:

  What do you think Jamaica is going to do?

  What will happen next?
- Visualizing:

  Make a picture in your mind of this scene.

  Can you see Jamaica pulling Kristin by the hand?
- Summarizing:

  What are the most important events in the story?
- Inferring:

  What are the motives that made Julia run away?

Promote the use of language prompts during the conversations after read aloud

Language prompts function as scaffolds to provide the language that children can use to express their thinking and participate in class discussions, sharing their ideas, agreeing and disagreeing, or providing support for their opinions. For a more detailed discussion of language prompts or sentence starters, see Chapter 2. *page 41*

After the Read Aloud

Facilitate conversation that deepens understanding of the book

All students benefit from conversations and discussions that deepen the understanding of the book being read. A whole-class conversation about a book can take place twice a week. Partner talk is also a powerful structure that enables questioning and clarifying different aspects of the book. During these periods in which students are talking and discussing, the teacher can assess and encourage the use of language prompts that promote thinking skills; children can evaluate, compare and contrast, share their opinions, and learn what the other students think about the book.

Specific Modifications for ELs and Struggling Students

In order for a Read Aloud to be used to its full potential, some specific modifications need to take place.

Before the read aloud

Preview the Book

It is very important to create a context for the students before you start reading the book (August & Shanahan, 2008). You may do a brief oral summary of the story and choose some of the most difficult words or idioms, and then give a short explanation of what they mean. If the read aloud is a continuation of the previous day, you can quickly review what you read before.

Julia, a fifth-grade teacher, said,

Teachers in the lower grades do picture walks before reading. The children have photographs, drawings, and pictures to remember what the book is about and what they read the day before. In the upper grades, many of the books that we read do not have pictures, so the summary that I make provides a context for the students.

Preteach Vocabulary

Choose only three to five key words to teach on any one day, words that double as new vocabulary words while representing the main components/tensions of the story. Teach the concepts behind the words, using illustrations, drama, gestures, synonyms, and putting them in the context of the story. Not a lot of talk! For example, we observed Luisa as she prepared her read aloud of *Shortcut* by Donald Crews (1992). She chose the words shortcut, train track, and train whistle to help the children understand the story. She used what she knew about her students to connect them to these words. For example, she started asking children if they took "shortcuts" when they walked to school.

Activate the Students' Previous Knowledge

As you introduce the book, ask students if they have had any previous experience reading books by the same author or with the same subject. For example, before reading *The Tortilla Factory* by Gary and Ruth Paulsen (1995), Luisa had a quick discussion about tortillas with her third-grade children and showed them different pictures from the book.

During the read aloud

Monitor for Comprehension Frequently

One of the best ways to model comprehension and to make sure that your students are accumulating information as the read aloud progresses is to monitor for comprehension:

- Stop periodically to summarize what has taken place so far in a story or to describe the information that has been learned.
- Provide opportunities for children to turn and talk throughout the book, prompting them with questions to help them process the information and organize their ideas, for example, *"Turn to your partner and summarize what we have read so far. Discuss with your partner what are the most important issues in this chapter."*

Use Language Scaffolds to Clarify Meaning

Definitions on the run. As you read and encounter a difficult word, define it quickly and then continue reading. For example, "The slaves were not considered autonomous individuals, *that means they were not considered free human beings.* They were considered property."

Paraphrasing. Use different words to be clearer when you read. Restate the phrase to provide an explanation. For example, "Tom's face got red and his eyes were bulging, *that means he was angry.*"

Rearranging syntax. When reading passages that may be confusing, insert a noun to clarify the meaning. For example, "After the Declaration of Independence, many Loyalists were ostracized. {They} *The Loyalists* had to go back to England."

[handwritten note: anaphora]

Give Children Time to Think About the Text and Answer Your Prompts

[handwritten note: Time to Think]

Provide time for students to process the questions and add an extra step so they can turn to their partners and discuss their answers.

After the read aloud

[handwritten note: Time to practice]

Work in small groups with the EL and struggling students, introducing the new language prompts you will be using during the read aloud and allowing them time to practice those prompts.

You need to do this every time you introduce new sentence starters or language prompts.

Spend Time Practicing the Language Prompts That Help Kids Conceptualize their Answers

It is particularly important to EL students to discuss, clarify, and expand their ideas through conversations and whole-class discussions. Table 3.1 summarizes the before-during-after process for read alouds. Also see the Template for Planning a Read Aloud at http://www.corwin.com/connectingcontent4ell.

Table 3.1   Template for Planning a Read Aloud for ELs and Struggling Students

Prior to the Read Aloud	During the Read Aloud	After the Read Aloud
Oral summary of the story Picture walk can illustrate the summary (if book has illustrations)	Think alouds	<ul><li>Focused partner and whole-group conversations that deepen comprehension of the text</li><li>Inside and outside retelling</li><li>Use higher level questions:<ul><li>*Synthesis:* "What would happen if . . . ?"</li><li>*Evaluation:* "Tell your partner what you think about. . . ."</li><li>*Knowledge:* "What happened after . . . ?"</li><li>*Analysis:* "Turn and tell your partner how would the ending have been if . . . happened."</li></ul></li></ul>
Choose only 3–5 key words to teach on any one day, words that double as new vocabulary words while representing the main components/tensions of the story. Teach the concepts behind the words using illustrations, drama, gestures, synonyms. Not a lot of talk! Use what you know about your students to connect them to these words. What do they know that can help them understand these words?	Add synonyms to clarify the meaning of words. If the text says, "It was *a splendid* day," read "splendid," then say "*beautiful.*" Tuck in definitions for unfamiliar words as one encounters them (*delightful*, that means *great*). Paraphrase instead of reading a section.	Recall the story using the initial 3–5 words. Reread the story or revisit it, this time perhaps teaching a few more vocabulary words. Again, 3–5 words, using methods described earlier.
	Rearrange syntax to clarify, inserting a noun in place of an indefinite pronoun. Instead of "it," she says, "the watermelon."	
Sometimes use very brief partner work to invite kids to "try on" the new words.	Three-way partnerships so that less fluent students can immerse themselves in language models.	
	Turn and talk—focus on comprehension and synthesis.	

SHARED READING

Best Practices for All Students

Decide the strategy you are going to teach, and choose the appropriate text

Shared reading has enormous potential as a teaching tool of reading and writing for struggling and EL students, because they learn best when exposed to explicit instruction in specific skills and strategies. The teacher models the strategy, and the students get the opportunity to practice without the pressure to perform in front of other students. The key to successful shared reading learning experiences is the selection of the text and planning the different strategies that you can teach in successive readings of the same text. This structure is an invaluable tool to teach and practice anything that needs revisiting, from punctuation to vocabulary, language structures, and text structures. The possibilities are endless.

It is very important that the text is large and that all students are able to see it as the teacher is reading. Students can have in their hand small copies of the text being read. Karen, a fifth-grade teacher, said, *"One of the most frustrating things that my students face is that the materials they can read are very childish and they do not relate to the interests of fifth graders that read at a third-grade level and below. During shared reading, I help them read texts that are above their reading level and texts that have sophisticated ideas. When I read with fluency and they follow along, I stop and make sure they have understood. Shared reading allows them to concentrate on the strategy I'm trying to teach. Then they go back to their tables and read the small booklets applying what they learned."*

State the purpose, telling kids the strategy you are going to teach or practice

Before you start, it is important to tell students the purpose of the shared reading activity. Letting students know what the lesson is going to be about and the strategy you are going to teach creates a context for the children; this is very important for second language learners. In addition, you need to tell them why this strategy is important. Rosa, a second-grade teacher, explained it this way: *"When I am using a big book for shared reading, I often do a picture walk to make sure that I tell my students what is the objective that I want them to concentrate on. I give them the teaching point. For example, I can say: 'Today we are going to pay particular attention to how the writer uses punctuation. Watch how my voice changes as I reach punctuation marks.'"*

At other times, you may provide a strategy focused on comprehension. For example, when reading nonfiction, you may say, *"It is really important that when we are reading a nonfiction text we stop after each section and make sure we understand what is the main idea. To show you what I mean, I'm going to read this page, which I have taken from our social studies textbook. Watch how I use sticky notes after each section to write down the main idea. After shared reading, I'm going to ask you to do the same in your booklets."*

Specific Modifications for ELs and Struggling Students

Connect the shared reading to the read aloud to recycle the language

You can use excerpts of the read aloud to provide students with a visual image of the language you have read. This is a form of exposing students to the same language in different formats: reading it (auditory) and seeing it written (visual). This gives the students more time to analyze language they have previously heard and to support language and content objectives.

Teach content language

Use shared reading to teach the language associated with the unit of study that you are working on. For example, if you are doing a unit on animal adaptations in science, you may do a shared reading activity that reflects the language from a text that the students will have to read. You can then spend time going over technical vocabulary that the students need to practice, such as *adaptations*, *environment*, *evolution*, and *extinct*.

Use shared reading to clarify science and social studies concepts

During shared reading, you can take a text explaining challenging concepts, such as the importance of the greenhouse effect on life on Earth, read it together with the group, and have a discussion with the students about the most important ideas.

Spend time analyzing language

During shared reading, you can read the same text several times for different purposes. In addition to teaching concepts, you can use the same texts to teach children strategies to understand complex language patterns such as relative clauses, complex verb tenses, and pronouns so that they can process these sentence structures when they read independently.

SHARED WRITING

Best Practices for All Students

Identify the purpose of the shared writing activity

Shared writing can serve many purposes, depending on the needs of the children. The students may need help with language conventions; they may need to clarify and sequence ideas; they may need to learn how to write in a particular genre. The teacher decides the context for the writing activity, and the content is decided collaboratively by the students and the teacher. Shared writing allows the students to experience the decision making that takes place when constructing an academic text. These decisions include word choice and linguistic structures that best fit the text that they are all creating together.

Write the text that has been collaboratively decided by the teacher and the students, emphasizing correct grammar and spelling

One of the most important characteristics of shared writing is that it models for students explicitly how oral language can be transformed into written language, at the same time that it clarifies notions about spelling and conventions of language. The students can see this connection because the text that the teacher is writing is based on their experiences; it reflects their own language as the teacher writes it, using correct grammar and spelling. This process is very helpful to students at all grade levels.

Specific Modifications for ELs and Struggling Students

Use a graphic organizer to help students plan the writing

Students benefit when you guide them to plan how they are going to organize the piece they are writing by using a semantic web (see more examples in Chapter 5). In the following example, Karen noticed that there was a group of students in her fifth-grade class who were having a hard time learning how to write book reviews. She pulled the group together, did a read aloud of Patricia Polacco's *Thank You Mr. Falker* (1998), and then did a shared writing activity to show the students how a book review is organized. She said to her students, *"Let's first organize our thoughts about the things we need to put in a book review, and then we can write it together. Pay attention because after this I will ask you to write your own book reviews. Right now, we will learn the components of a book review."* As the students offered suggestions under her guidance, she listed them in the web using correct syntax (see Figure 3.2).

Figure 3.2   Web for Shared Writing

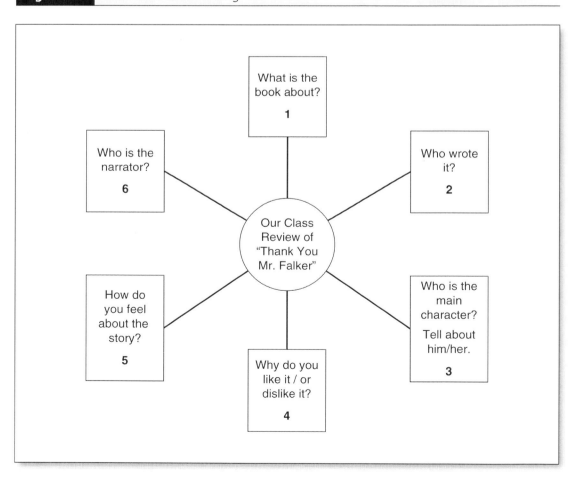

After much discussion, the students collectively wrote the following review (see box).

> *"Thank You Mr. Falker" is a story about a little girl that feels very sad. It was written by Patricia Polacco. The main character is a girl named Tricia. She has problems reading and writing, and she has a hard time until her fifth grade teacher helps her. We really liked it because at the end she can learn. We feel that sometimes we have problems like her. The narrator is the girl: she is Patricia Polacco. This is her story.*

Focus on the development of academic language

For ELs and struggling learners, the most important characteristic of shared writing is that it helps them to write texts that are more complex than what they could do independently. The students may express a thought in simple terms, and the teacher may show them a more sophisticated way of expressing and writing the thought enriching their vocabulary and grammar in the process.

Recycle shared writing into a shared reading activity

The shared writing text that was created collectively by all the students and the teacher can be "recycled" to become a shared reading text. By reinforcing and practicing the language portrayed in the text, the students will become more familiar and comfortable with it, and will incorporate it into their oral discourse faster.

Tables 3.3 through 3.5 summarize the best practices for read aloud shared reading and shared writing and the recommended additions to support the development of academic language in ELs.

Best Practices

Table 3.3 Read Aloud Best Practices

Read Aloud Best Practices	Additions for ELs and Struggling Students
1. Plan specific objectives and the work you will do as you select the text 2. Become very familiar with the book before the read aloud 3. Model reading strategies through think alouds 4. Promote the use of language prompts during the conversation after the read aloud	1. Preview book 2. Preteach vocabulary 3. Activate the students' previous knowledge 4. Use language scaffolds to clarify meaning 5. Monitor for comprehension frequently 6. Give children time to think and answer—turn to partners and discuss their answers 7. Spend time introducing and practicing the language prompts that help kids conceptualize their answers

Table 3.4 Shared Reading Best Practices

Shared Reading Best Practices	Additions for ELs and Struggling Students
1. Decide the strategy you are going to teach, and choose the appropriate text 2. State the purpose, telling kids the strategy you are going to teach or practice 3. Read the text, inviting children to read at specific times	1. Teaching content language 2. Connect to read aloud to recycle the language 3. Use shared reading to clarify science or social studies concepts 4. Spend time analyzing language

Table 3.5 Shared Writing Best Practices

Shared Writing Best Practices	Additions for ELs and Struggling Students

1. Identify the purpose of the shared writing activity:
  a. Use of language conventions
  b. How to organize thoughts into writing
2. Teacher writes text dictated by students with correct grammar and spelling
	1. Focus on academic language
	2. Use of graphic organizer to plan writing
	3. A shared writing can become the shared reading activity

CONCLUSION

Balanced literacy structures offer many opportunities for students to engage in the process of learning through talk and collaboration in reading and writing activities. In this chapter, we have offered suggestions of ways you can modify some of the structures of balanced literacy to support the development of language and literacy in EL and struggling students. These students flourish under the structures of balanced literacy when teachers make modifications that reinforce the development of academic language throughout the day and throughout the unit.

QUESTIONS FOR REFLECTION

Try to answer as many questions as you can:

1. How does your own philosophy of literacy fit with the philosophy of balanced literacy?

2. What additional modifications would you add to the structures of balanced literacy that we present in this chapter, in order to support ELs and struggling students?

3. The structures of Read Aloud, Shared Reading, and Shared Writing allow the child to learn language (versus acquiring language in Krashen's [1997] terms). Can you explain why? Can you think of other classrooms instances where you could support language learning and acquisition?

PART II

The Lesson Component

Sample Units to Integrate Content and Language Goals

The challenge for teachers of second language learners is a complex one: Students need to understand the content of a unit, but they don't have all the language that is required to learn it. The planning for the units we will share in the next four chapters reflects our belief that the most effective way to teach a second language is by using a context (a unit of study) in deliberate ways so that we teach the language at the same time that we teach content. Within this context, we embed the thinking skills as well as the language structures the unit requires. Children will learn new language structures in the process of learning the content. In this way, language is used and learned as a vehicle of communication, not as an end in itself.

When we plan lessons for EL children, we must assess and refine background knowledge and pay attention to the development of critical thinking skills and academic language. Teachers who are not accustomed to thinking purposely about language development struggle with these three essential elements. While it is easy to include vocabulary as the language objective, it is more difficult to identify the needed language structures and thinking skills.

Learning the language that goes with the unit becomes an important goal, but it is not enough; we must also spend time developing the background knowledge that children must have in order to integrate the new knowledge.

4

Language Arts Unit

Memoir (Grades 3–6)

This chapter is divided in two sections, which aim to accomplish the following:

Section 1

- focus on storytelling about families, as a way to connect children to the meaning of *memoir*;
- anchor the unit in *interactive read aloud* as a tool for developing background knowledge and critical thinking skills;
- provide templates for planning the unit;
- provide templates for planning *interactive read alouds*; and
- use whole-class and small-group conversations to anchor the concepts and language learned.

Section 2

- address the specific language goals in developing the students' academic language.

INTRODUCTION

The purpose of the *memoir* unit of study is to get students to explore their lives and gather universal meaning as they write about people, places, and events that have particular meaning for them (Bomer, 2005; Calkins, 1994). For EL students, the memoir unit is an opportunity to examine their own lives and experiences for meaning and to incorporate those experiences into their writing. What makes memoir a special genre is that it is a look at the past in order to try to draw meaning from it. For example, a child may write about his memory of his first experience in school as he stepped into his kindergarten class. He describes the anxiety and excitement he felt as he reluctantly said goodbye to his mother standing at the door of his classroom. As he reflects on the experience, he finds a larger meaning in it and uses it as a metaphor for the unsettling feelings we have when we begin to move away from our mothers and towards independence.

Memoirs are very personal reflections. Somebody else cannot write your memoir or it would be a biography, and it cannot be chronological or it would be an autobiography. Getting the children to understand the difference between these three types of writing is essential, and it is equally important to help them understand the reflective characteristics of memoir. In a memoir, you interpret a memory (Bomer, 2005).

[handwritten: 7 definitions]

SECTION 1: THE ENGLISH LANGUAGE LEARNER AND MEMOIR

Ms. Lago's class of fifth graders has 27 students, including three newcomers and nine other English language learners at different stages of language acquisition. The native languages of the ELs are Spanish, Bengali, Haitian Creole, and Cantonese. In addition, several of her English-dominant students are struggling learners, in that they have either academic or emotional issues that interfere with their academic success. An ESL teacher works with the EL students three times per week as a ***push in teacher*** (inside the classroom) during the literacy period. The ESL teacher uses her time with the children to help scaffold the language arts content that children must acquire. She plans what she is going to teach by following the classroom teacher's plans for the unit.

Ms. Lago generally teaches this unit in the middle of the school year, after the children have been immersed in other literary genres such as personal narrative, personal essay, and poetry. Memoirs can be written in one or a combination of these genres, so children need to know how to write in all of them. The teacher had taught this unit before, but in previous years she did not have as many ELs in her classroom, and her students were better prepared to deal with the abstract concepts this genre presents. This year, the teacher was concerned that many of her students were going to face challenges as they strove to understand the concepts of the unit. Students would be asked to reflect on a particular experience and interpret its meaning as they wrote their own memoirs, and thus they needed to understand the meaning of metaphor to grasp the real concept of memoir. The memory becomes a metaphor that expresses the message the author is conveying. This unit asks children to think deeply, to reflect and draw meaning from their experiences; many ELs and struggling students may not have the language to accomplish this.

Although Ms. Lago was concerned about getting her children to grasp the content of the unit and to write their memoirs with depth and rich language, she saw, at the same time, an opportunity to develop academic language and critical thinking skills in her students.

The teacher's concern was based on the struggles that her students were having during the reading period. Ms. Lago had organized the students into five groups, according to their reading level, which she determined by a reading assessment that is used by the district and that she administered early in September. Each group read a different book, which approximated their reading level. Since she was working on the Memoir unit for her language arts period, each group was reading a different memoir. She tried to work with every group for at least 15 minutes every day, while the children in the other groups did independent reading or discussed the book they were reading. She noticed that when she was not working directly with the group, most of the children had a hard time talking about the text. When she listened

[handwritten: 5 groups]

to the conversations that her students were having, they were mostly about details in the narrative that had no connection with the critical aspects of the texts that she outlined.

During one of our early meetings with Ms. Lago, she wondered if there was a way that she could help her students to delve deeper into the text and develop critical thinking skills by asking "better" questions. This brought us into a discussion of the kinds of critical thinking skills and language that children would need in order to hold meaningful classroom talk for the Memoir unit. The teacher then decided that as she planned this unit, she would need to develop a plan for how classroom talk would be the venue to develop critical thinking skills. We came up with a set of critical thinking skills following Bloom's *Taxonomy* (1956) that reflected what she wanted her students to accomplish in this particular unit of study: comprehension, analysis, evaluation, and synthesis. She included these skills in her plan for classroom talk, which guided the conversation prompts she used during class conversations throughout the unit.

To prepare her students to deal with the content, the teacher added 2 weeks at the front end to develop the background knowledge and language that the students needed. Ms. Lago believed that in order for her students to understand the purpose of writing a personal memoir, she needed to plan how to address the different content and language challenges that her students would face as she progressed through the unit. She used a ***planning template*** (see Table 4.1) that helped her make sure that she was addressing the needs of her students, including

- developing background knowledge;
- curriculum of talk: critical thinking skills; and
- language development through ***read aloud*** and ***shared reading***.

Theory-to-Practice Connection

Background knowledge represents what we know about the world; it also affects how we learn new information, how we store it, and how we remember it. For more information, see Chapter 1.

Talk is a key element in the process of learning and has to be an integral part of the plan for the unit. See Chapter 2.

Shared reading and read aloud allow the teacher to model academic language. See Chapter 3.

Ms. Lago used a myriad of activities to develop concepts, language, and syntactic structures to support her students as she planned her units of study. We suggest that you follow Ms. Lago's idea of spending 2 weeks getting her EL and struggling students ready before she introduced the unit to the rest of the class. You should choose the activities that will work better for your specific population. (see the Unit Planning Chart at http://www.corwin.com/connectingcontent4ell).

BREAKING THE PLAN INTO DOABLE PARTS

Immersion in Concepts and Language Through Read Aloud and Shared Reading

Prior to starting the unit with the class, Ms. Lago started working in small groups with her EL students and struggling students, exposing them to a lot of memoirs during read aloud, while

Table 4.1 Planning Template for Memoir Unit of Study

Background Knowledge	Curriculum of Talk: Thinking Skills	Language Development
Storytelling of Family Memories	*Kinds of Questions That Will Guide Our Thinking*	*Read Aloud, Shared Reading*
Reflections about important people and places in children's lives: • Heart map • Graphic organizers	*Analysis* • Why do you think . . . ? • What were the reasons for . . . ? • How would you change . . . ? *Comprehension* • Tell in your own words. • Describe how you feel about . . . • Compare . . . with . . . *Synthesis* • What might have happened if . . . ? • What ideas can you add? *Evaluation* • Do you agree with . . . ? • What do you think about . . . ?	• Vocabulary • Pronoun substitutions • Figurative language: *Metaphors* "I was the shadow in the moonlight." *Similes* "His voice was as loud as a siren."
Immersion through ***read alouds***: • Rylant & Gammell (1985): *The Relatives Came* • Donald Crews (1992): *Shortcut* • Yolen & Schoenherr (2007): *Owl Moon*		
Graphic organizers to connect children to books: • Reflecting on important people and places in our lives • Reflecting on books	**Language Prompts**	
	Analysis • I think that . . . because . . . • The reasons for . . . are . . . • I would change . . . • I would add . . . *Comprehension* • I think that . . . • What comes to my mind is . . . • This is the way I feel about . . . • On the one hand. . . . On the other . . .	
Provide collection of memoirs for read aloud	*Synthesis* • I have learned that . . . • I can also think of . . . *Evaluation* • I agree (or disagree) with . . . because . . . • In my opinion . . .	

at the same time developing vocabulary and creating a context for the main concepts she would later teach. She also asked the ESL teacher to do some of this work with her EL students. At the start of the unit, she gave the ESL teacher some of the read aloud mentor texts, so that she could do second readings with the children and work on the language challenges that those books presented. The teacher knew that her ELs needed to hear the books several times and listen to the rich language repeatedly in order to integrate the new vocabulary and concepts.

Ms. Lago used interactive read aloud to develop background knowledge and used shared reading to develop vocabulary and to work on syntax and other language structures. Through the conversations she facilitated, the teacher helped students develop critical thinking skills and practice the language structures they were acquiring throughout the unit.

As we have discussed in a previous chapter, ***read aloud*** and ***shared reading*** are very important structures that teachers can use as tools to develop language and literacy in ELs and struggling students. Read aloud and ***accountable talk*** are not just opportunities to read and discuss a book, but also an opportunity to understand with the help of others. They provide children with language input and with the opportunity to talk about the text with other children. Often children mimic the language forms they hear from more proficient speakers. Read alouds give teachers the opportunity to read books that EL children can't access on their own and to introduce sophisticated language they don't usually hear. Shared reading is a teaching tool that shows children how reading and writing work. Through this experience, children learn not only new vocabulary but also new language structures and syntax.

Assessing and Developing Background Knowledge

Many teachers tell us that the memoir genre is a particularly difficult unit for ELs. This is why we have decided to focus on it. We believe that all children can draw from their own life stories and find a particular experience that has made an impact in their lives and reflect on who they are as people. The challenge for teachers is to guide them to find meaning in those experiences and to help them learn the language to express themselves.

Ms. Lago wanted the children to generate ideas for writing memoirs through the use of their own stories. Most children come from families that have stories that have survived a long time and are part of the conversations with relatives when they get together at gatherings. We seldom tap into this extraordinary well of information. What we mean by a family's stories are the traditions of oral narrative that families share passed through several generations, often told with variations. These are stories of valor under difficult circumstances, compassion in very trying times, funny moments that the family relishes, and more. These are part of the repertoires of many families. The students can also generate ideas by looking at family picture albums, asking their parents to tell them how they chose their names or how their parents met. Storytelling within this context not only helps students connect with their own family histories, but it helps the students to learn how to use language and share coherent stories with other children. The new arrivals were encouraged to share their stories in their native language, to make an illustration describing a particular part of their lives, or to share a special item they brought from their country.

Ms. Lago initiated the storytelling by gathering the class at the meeting place and saying,

I see that today you brought lots of stories about your families. So let's get organized and figure out how we are going to conduct this conversation . . . mmm . . . let's write a little conversation guide for us so that we can really hear each other and ask smart questions of each other.

She wrote on a chart, adding suggestions from the children.
When we are telling our stories:

- We listen to each other.
- We make eye contact with the speaker when we ask a question.
- We ask questions only if we want to learn something new or if we did not understand something the storyteller said.

- Before we tell the story, we ask ourselves, "Why do I think this is an important story?"
- Here are some language prompts we can use to help us with our telling:
  - ○ I am going to tell you a story about. . . .
  - ○ This story makes me think about. . . .

Theory-to-Practice Connection

The teacher is setting up the ground rules for carrying out a literate conversation. See Chapter 2.

She started the process by modeling her own story:

I am going to tell you a story about my name. I asked my mother why my two names are Soledad Luna. She told me that the night she went into premature labor (this means when I decided it was time to come into this world) my father was working a late shift and she was alone in the house. As she sat in a chair on the porch waiting for my aunt to pick her up to take her to the hospital, she felt really lonely, and, at some point, she looked up and saw a full moon! When I was finally born after many hours of labor, my mother knew that my name would have to be Soledad (in English, loneliness) Luna (moon).

She stopped and waited for the students to ask a question.

Lorena   Why is this story important?

Ms. Lago   I think this story is important because now I can understand why I have such a weird combination of names. I could really write about this in my memoir! I can see my mother sitting there in the dark. . . . Good question!

Ms. Lago   Now that you have heard me telling my story, let's start now with your own stories.

Pedro   I am going to tell you a story about something sad. I asked my father what was the sadder time for him, and he said when we had to go to Puerto Rico to see my grandma because she was sick, very sick, and my father and my mother and my sister and me went to Puerto Rico, and it was very hot, like 100 degrees, and I was a baby and they had to change my clothes. Then, we went to see my grandma in the hospital and she was sleeping, and sleeping. She won't get up. My father was sad.

Madeleine   Was she dead?

Pedro   Yes.

Other children contributed their stories and attempted to follow the conversation guidelines. In addition to serving as a bridge to connect with the memoir genre, this activity allowed the students to share their lives, culture, and family traditions with the rest of the class.

Helping Children Access Their Memories

Another way in which Ms. Lago helped her fifth graders think about meaningful memories was by getting them to work on a graphic organizer, or a ***heart map***. This was the first step in getting her students to write a memoir. They must first access their own experiences so that they later can reflect on the meaning and impact those memories had on their lives. This activity helped the children realize that they have valuable life experiences that they can write about. Many children do not think that their personal experiences can be used in school settings.

The children in Ms. Lago's class were paired in ***three-way partnerships***. Three-way partnerships consist of an EL, a bilingual learner, and an English-dominant academic proficient student. This means that every EL who needs more support in English is paired with a student who is more proficient in English, so that he or she can negotiate meaning, and with an English-dominant student who can move the conversation along. This gives all the children opportunities to brainstorm about important events, people, and places that have had particular impact on their lives and made them who they are. Through these three-way partnerships, every child, including the more recent arrivals, can participate in the conversations. Ms. Lago modeled this activity for her students by adding important people and places in her own heart map or graphic organizer. This made the process very visual for the students. Then, she got the children to practice with their partners what they would place in their heart, before they put their ideas on paper. Some of her guiding questions included:

- What memory stands out that involves your family and friends?
- If you close your eyes and think of special moments or events, what are the moments that you see first with your heart?
- Can you think of some special memories that had a particular impact on you?

Figure 4.2   Madeleine's Heart Map

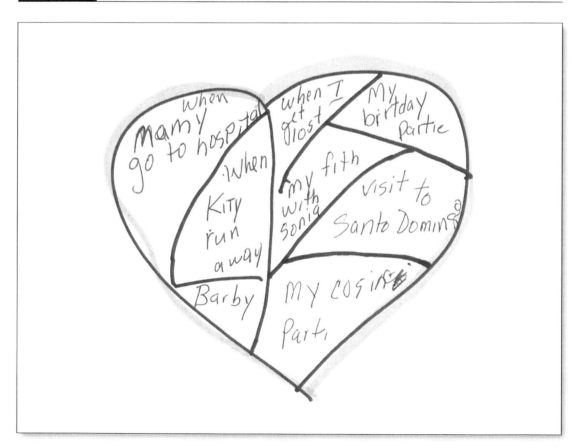

After giving the children time to work on their hearts (see Figure 4.2 for an example), Ms. Lago asked the children to select the most meaningful memory and try to remember details about it. The children took some time to select the memory they wanted to work on and began to expand on what they remembered.

Figure 4.3   Madeleine's First Notebook Entry

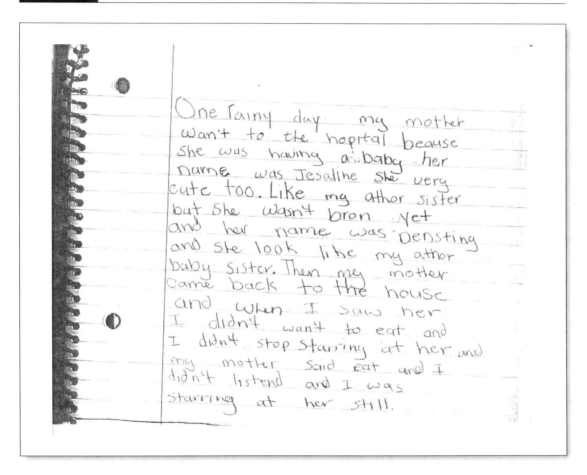

Madeleine's first entry in her notebook (see Figure 4.3) was an attempt at collecting a memory about the birth of her sister, trying to remember details of what happened, particularly her reaction the first time she saw her sister.

The teacher then asked the students to do a timeline so that they could add more details to their memories (see Figure 4.4).

Ms. Lago used this opportunity to focus her students on the meaning of their memories. She made a list of the topics (see Table 4.5) that her students chose and prompted them to explain why these topics were important to them.

Through this activity, the teacher got her students to think purposefully about their memories and to interpret their memories and what they meant. This work continued throughout interactive read alouds and other activities connected to the mentor texts she read.

Figure 4.4   Rosario's Timeline

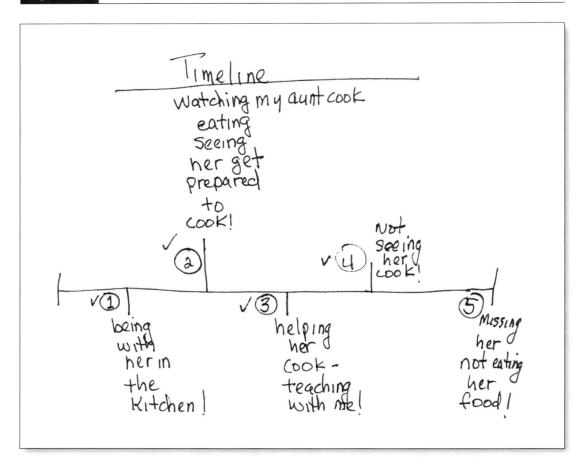

Table 4.5   Our Memories

Our Memories	Why I Think This Is Important to Me
Our apartment fire. *(Juan)*	We lost our furniture, I was scared.
My mother going to the hospital. *(Madeleine)*	We had a baby sister, I was very happy.
My grandma's funeral. *(Malva)*	She always took care of me. I did not have anyone to take care of me.
Time I spent with my aunt in the kitchen watching her cook and eating her food. *(Rosario)*	She gave me good advice. I miss her a lot and feel sad she is dead.

Theory-to-Practice Connection

In addition to planning activities to access background knowledge, the teacher has used a graphic organizer to help students clarify their ideas. See Chapter 1.

IMMERSION IN THE GENRE THROUGH READ ALOUD

Anchor the unit of study in read alouds. Read lots of memoirs. This will help the children to understand the structure of the genre. For EL children, it is probable that you and your ESL teacher will read the same books more than once. You will need to choose books that convey the meaning of memoir without language density, so we suggest you use picture memoir books as they have a lot of visual support for ELs. We like to start with books like *A Chair for My Mother* by Vera Williams (1982) and *Shortcut* by Donald Crews (1992) because the children may have heard them before in the early grades, so they have a good sense of the story. The beautiful books you will read as you move along in the unit, like Eloise Greenfield's (with L. Jones, P. Jones, & J. Pinkney) *Childtimes* (1979), Cynthia Rylant's (with S. Gammell) *The Relatives Came* (1985), Jorge Argueta's *La Fiesta de las Tortillas* (2006), or Sandra Cisneros's *The House on Mango Street* (1991), will offer EL children many opportunities to connect with the themes and to remember episodes of their own lives.

As we mentioned before, some kids enjoy multiple readings of the same book. This is a very enriching practice since the students know the books and the language but the multiple exposures will allow them to look for different elements that you want them to think about

- an event or series of events; and
- their significance for the writer.

How does the author experience the event as he or she looks back? How does he or she interpret the events now?

A read aloud for ELs needs to be modified to address the children's cognitive and linguistic challenges. We suggest that teachers use a template (see Table 4.6) to plan some of their read alouds, so that they can make sure that they are not only working on comprehension skills, but also on language structures and vocabulary, and on higher order thinking.

Table 4.6 Template for Read Aloud of *Shortcut* by Donald Crews

Prior to the Read Aloud	During the Read Aloud (Scaffolds)	After the Read Aloud
A summary generally integrates the elements of story. This should not take more than 3 minutes. Summary of text: This book is about the writer and his friends. He remembers an episode in his life when they decided to go home the short way and got into a scary situation by walking on the train tracks. If you speak the language of the children, you can do this summary in the native language.	*Think Alouds* During read aloud, the teacher models the thinking a good reader is apt to do as he or she reads. This makes me think . . . I am wondering what a shortcut means. I wonder why they took a shortcut.	Focused partner and whole-group conversations that deepen comprehension of the text. Example of questions for the Read Aloud of *Shortcut:* What made the kids so afraid? Do you think that the children made a good decision by taking the shortcut? *Synthesis* "What would happen if. . . ." *Evaluation* "Tell your partner what you think about . . ."

(Continued)

Table 4.6 (Continued)

	Use chart to list key concepts and vocabulary. Students should take notes: Key Words in *Shortcut* • shortcut • railroad tracks • passenger train • freight train • mound • slopes • tussled • cut-off	*Knowledge* "What happened after . . ." *Analysis* "Turn and tell your partner how would the ending have been if. . . . happened."
Choose 3–5 key words to teach on any one day. Teach the concepts behind the words using illustrations, drama, gestures, synonyms. *Shortcut* Use what you know about your students to connect them to this word. "This means you take the shortest way to get somewhere. Have you ever taken a *shortcut?*" What do they know that can help them understand this word? Other words to work on: • track • passenger trains • freight trains • train whistle	Add synonyms to clarify the meaning of words. i.e. railroad tracks, the place (rails) where trains run, slopes, little hills	Reread the story or revisit it, this time perhaps teaching a few more vocabulary words. Again, 3–5 words, using methods described earlier.
	Re-arrange syntax to clarify, inserting a noun in place of an indefinite pronoun. Instead of "it," say, "the whistle of the train."	
Use very brief partner work to invite kids to "try on" the new words. They should make sentences and be encouraged to use the new words in oral and written language.	Use 3 way partnerships so less fluent students can immerse themselves in language models. Turn and talk: focus on comprehension and synthesis.	Partner work using vocabulary words. Story mountain

Theory-to-Practice Connection

The teacher has structured the read aloud with modifications, in order to support the development of language and literacy in her EL and struggling students. See Chapter 3.

DEVELOPING KNOWLEDGE ABOUT THE GENRE AFTER READING MANY MEMOIRS

Ms. Lago noticed a significant problem. Even after reading several memoirs, some of the children were still having a hard time differentiating between a personal narrative and a memoir that has a larger meaning. Children were writing about things that happened to them, but were having a harder time interpreting the meaning of their memory. In order to help the students understand this critical aspect of the genre, Ms. Lago spent time during interactive read aloud to point out the characteristics of the memoir genre, so that the children could understand how it works and could pinpoint the elements of memoir as they read or listened to the books. She had chart paper next to her as she read and, as children discovered the different elements of the genre, she listed them. For example, she listed the following items

[handwritten margin note: Memoirs have meaning / interpret the meaning]

- the writer is always the main character of the memoir; and
- memoirs always involve an event in the past.

After she completed several interactive read alouds, the teacher organized the children in groups and asked them to develop a *concept definition map* of what a memoir is. This activity elicited a discussion that would help the children think about the difference between the memoir genre and other genres and synthesize information.

Ms. Lago	From the books that we have read, what are the common elements of the genre?
Marlene	They are stories.
Pedro	Like when you are really scared or happy and you always remember that for the rest of your life.
Lucia	You learn something from that, it stays with you.
Rosario	It's like in a memoir you tell the story and then you tell what you learn.
Ms. Lago	How are memoirs different from other kinds of writing?
Madeleine	It is something that really happened to us, like when my sister was born and how I felt.
Gloria	It is different that books that tell you about things, like when we write reports.

Figure 4.7 shows an example of one of the concept definition maps for memoir that the students developed.

Figure 4.7   Concept Definition Map of Memoir

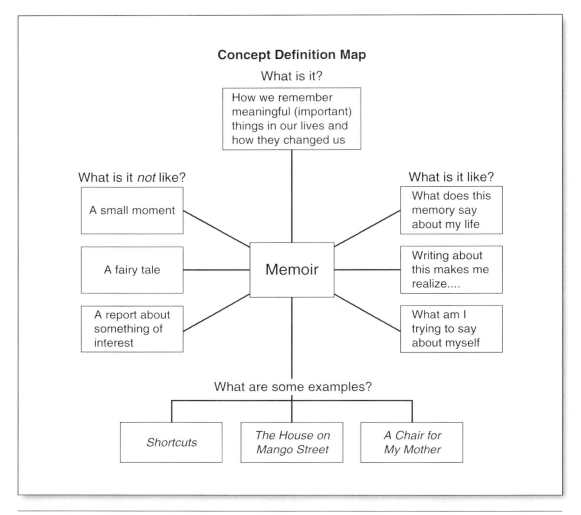

Source: Based on Buehl (2009).

In order to connect to the mentor texts and to their own memories, children in Ms. Lago's class needed time to think about their feelings and the feelings that the books they were reading were triggering. The graphic organizer shown in Table 4.8 helped them explore ideas for their own memories. As they thought about the important people and places in their lives, they reflected on the ones that had the most meaning.

Table 4.8   Graphic Organizer for Exploring Memories

Reflecting on Important People and Places in Our Lives			
Places and people that are important (meaningful) to me	What did I feel there?	What made this an important place/person?	What was the important lesson?

One of the strategies that Ms. Lago used to convey concepts without the overload of a lot of language was to use graphic organizers to help children think critically about the books she read, so that they could comprehend the essence of these memoirs. She knew that she needed to be very explicit with most of her children so that they truly understood how the author developed his memoir. She did not do this with every book, but she did it when the children needed to dwell more deeply on the books and establish connections that were going to help them use those reflections in their own writing.

After reading *Shortcut* (Crews, 1992) and *Owl Moon* (Yolen & Schoenherr, 2007), Ms. Lago gave the children graphic organizers to help them think about the books and how they related to their own lives (see Tables 4.9 and 4.10).

Table 4.9   Reflecting on *Shortcut*

What are the children feeling?	What was the setting?	What was the lesson they learned	How did Donald Crews show impending disaster?
Have you ever been in a situation when you felt the same way?	Where were you?	What lesson did you learn?	How are you going to describe this in your writing?

Table 4.10   Reflecting on *Owl Moon*

What are the "rules" people must follow when they go owling?	Why were the rules important?	What was special about the setting?	What can you infer about the relationship between the child and the father?
Have you ever been in a situation when you have to follow rules that require "special" behavior from you?	Why was it important that you follow the rules?	Where did this happen and how did you feel?	What can you write about your relationship with one of your family members?

After every read aloud, there was always a whole class discussion so that children could synthesize the major concepts of the book.

After reading *Shortcut*, Ms. Lago had a whole classroom conversation. The children were seated in a circle. The teacher had a chart with conversation prompts that she pushed the children to use during ***accountable talk***:

- "I think that . . ."
- "This is the way I feel about . . ."
- "In my opinion . . ."
- "I agree (or disagree) because . . ."

Ms. Lago	So, after reading this book, what are the questions that we have? Let's make a list.
Ms. Lago	My first question is: What is this book about?
Ms. Lago	Do you have the same question? Turn to the person next to you and tell them the questions you have.

The children had a lively discussion with their partners.

Ms. Lago	So, what are your questions?
Juan	Why did they take a shortcut?
Jose	Why where they afraid?

Ms. Lago added the questions to her chart.

Ms. Lago	Any other questions? So let's start with my question.
Madeleine	The story is about a some children. They went for a walk and then they decide to take a shortcut.
Jose	That was the problem. They took the shortcut . . . and. . . .
Luisa	They were scared because they were almost killed by a train.
Rosario	You answered the other question! That was the memory . . . how the kids were really scared. That was the time in his life when they . . . really . . . really scared.
Lucia	They were afraid to. . . .
Madeleine	Tell!!!
Ms. Lago	Mmmm . . . good points. So the book is about one incident that happened. . . . But remember to use the language prompts.
Ms. Lago	(Showing illustrations from the book:) Who is writing this memoir?
Consuelo	I think that one of the children, but he is old now.
Ms. Lago	Good! You used a language prompt! You mean older.
Ms. Lago	What makes this a memoir and not just a story?
K'Lene	In my opinion, this tells a true thing that did happen.
Michael	They thought that it was OK to do it, that they would be safe.
Abdul	That nothing . . . happen.
Jean Marie	The writer is thinking about the time when he and his friends were almost killed by a train . . . and how scared it is.
Madeleine	And also it is a memoir because he remembers and writes. . . .
Ms. Lago	(Pointing to the language prompts:) How could you say that in a more complete way?
Madeleine	I agree because he remembers. . . .
Ms. Lago	Excellent work. Turn to your partner and take turns in retelling the story.

Theory-to-Practice Connection

Language prompts are sentence starters that help students use higher order thinking skills. See Chapter 2.

While her students were retelling, the teacher worked with her two recent arrivals. She asked them to tell her what the book was all about (they had already worked with the book in their ESL period) and wrote down what the students said. She allowed them to look at the pictures, to use their native language to complete their thoughts, and to draw pictures that tell the summary.

In this part, we have shown you how through read aloud you can develop a knowledge base for your EL students. In this way, you can provide a road map that will help the children recognize the key elements of the genre and to use some of their personal memories to start reflecting on the feelings that were elicited.

SECTION 2: ADDRESSING LANGUAGE NEEDS

Vocabulary

Ms. Lago told us that she always planned her vocabulary work by asking herself: "What is the new vocabulary that is essential for EL children to understand in order to get the full meaning of the mentor texts I am using?" She also thought about the vocabulary that was essential for the unit; words like *reflection, memoir, memorable.* Then, she developed a plan of action for how she was going to teach the new words and concepts and figured out how she would provide opportunities for the children to incorporate the new words into their speaking and writing.

This implies that she needed to review the books for possible words that might have been challenging and select those words that were central to understanding the meaning of the memoir. Vocabulary related to the mentor texts she planned on using depended on the mentor book choices she made. As she introduced the unit, she worked mainly with four mentor texts to develop vocabulary and to teach new syntactic structures: *Owl Moon, Shortcut, A Chair for My Mother,* and *The House on Mango Street.*

Looking at vocabulary in this way allows the teacher to organize her thinking and gives her a road map on how to proceed to figure out an appropriate strategy for teaching the new words and expressions. It also helps her to limit the number of words she is going to teach (see Tables 4.11 and 4.12).

Theory-to-Practice Connection

Language development has to be planned carefully and integrated into the plans for the unit. These planning charts show how the teaching of vocabulary will be incorporated in the unit and the strategies the teacher will use. See Chapter 1.

Table 4.11 Vocabulary From *Shortcut*

Vocabulary From *Shortcut*	Strategy	Where Do I Teach It?
• Tracks • Freight trains • Whistle • Schedule • Passenger train • Tussled • Cut-off • Mound	Definitions on the run Word sorts Word webs (with related words)	• During read aloud • We can preteach some words before we begin the read aloud Shared reading Word study
Feeling Words • Fear • Anxiety • Panic	• Word webs (with related words) • Create a chart with "shades of feelings" (from *relaxed* to *panicky*)	Refer to it during interactive read aloud, or as part of our word study

Table 4.12 Vocabulary From *Owl Moon*

Vocabulary From *Owl Moon*	Strategy	Where Do I teach It?
• Owling • Woolen cap • Our feet crunched • Long shadow • Pine trees • Great horned owl • Furry mouth • Hooted • Stared • Pumped its great wings	Definitions on the run Word webs (with related words)	During read aloud We can also preteach some words before we begin the read aloud Shared reading Word study
Similes and Metaphors • The trees stood still as giant statues • Quiet as a dream	Simile and metaphor word wall Venn diagrams	Word study

Many of the children in Ms. Lago's class had a very poor knowledge of vocabulary. Their writing was stilted and predictable. To enrich their vocabulary and get children to remember the new words they were learning, the teacher knew that it was important to present new vocabulary in a cluster of related words. This not only helps in understanding the target word but also facilitates retrieving the word and using it. She decided that the Memoir unit was a good place to develop vocabulary that describes feelings.

After reading *Shortcut* by Crews, she started her vocabulary work:

Ms. Lago   Let's think about how the children in the story felt when they heard the train coming closer and closer to them.

Pedro   They were nervous.

Ms. Lago	(Writing on chart paper:) The children in *Shortcut* were nervous when the train came. Can we think of another word instead of nervous?
Madeleine	Fear?
Ms. Lago	Yes! Let's make a web with these words (see Figure 4.13).

Figure 4.13 Word Web of *Nervous*

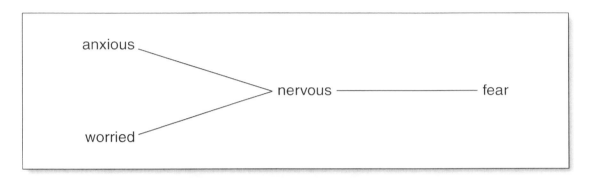

Ms. Lago	Can we think of other words that mean the same as nervous?
Madeleine	Afraid.
Ms Lago	Well, fear and afraid are the same word. Fear is what you feel when you are afraid. Let's think about another word.

(No response)

| Ms. Lago | How do you feel before you take the ELA test? |

Students in unison: "Anxious."

| Ms. Lago | So, now we know that the kids in *Shortcut* felt anxious and they were nervous and felt fear. |

This web presents a cluster of related words, of which the students may know some. Even though they are not exact synonyms, they are closely related in meaning.

The teacher got students to use the new word in sentences. Using a prompt facilitated this task:

I feel anxious when _____.

I have experienced fear when _____.

The new word was placed on the word wall together with other words associated with the unit. Ms. Lago also used other activities, which we have discussed in previous chapters, such as word sorts, shades of meanings, and others, to expand the vocabulary of this unit.

Through all the vocabulary activities that she presented to her students, Ms. Lago hoped to enable them to assimilate the new language they were learning into their repertoire, as they were organizing words in clusters, and to enable an understanding of the relationship between words and their synonyms.

Theory-to-Practice Connection

The best way to ensure that children will incorporate new words into their repertoire is by providing them with opportunities to use them, by clustering them with associated words, and by prompting the children to use them during classroom discussions. See Chapter 1.

Deepening Word Knowledge Through Definitions on the Run and Word Walls

In read aloud, we use definitions on the run to explain words students may not understand. To deepen our students' knowledge of those words, we suggest a *word wall* that can be specific to the writing unit of study—the teacher as well as children can add to the wall as new words are learned during read aloud or independent reading. Keeping tabs on how those words are used in the daily life of the students will help students incorporate the new vocabulary into their repertoire.

ELEMENTS OF COHESION

Pronoun Substitution

Many EL students get confused by **anaphoras**, or sentences that have pronoun substitutions (see Chapter 1 for examples). Pronouns play a key role in linking sentences together. We have to know exactly whom the pronoun is substituting for; usually, pronouns point to a referent or (noun) that has already been mentioned.

The shared reading activity illustrated in Figure 4.14 gives the students a strategy to figure out whom the pronoun refers to.

Figure 4.14   *A Chair for My Mother* by Vera Williams (1982)

My mother works as a waitress in the Blue Tile Diner. After school sometimes I go to meet her there. Then her boss Josephine gives me a job too.

It takes a long time to fill a jar this big. Every day when my mother comes home from work, I take down the jar. My mama empties all her change from tips out of her purse for me to count. Then we push all of the coins into the jar.

In this activity, children need to figure out whom the pronouns refer to. You can cover the pronouns with a sticky note and ask the children to substitute either the noun or the pronoun. You can also draw arrows linking the pronoun with the noun, as in the example above.

Theory-to-Practice Connection

Here is an example of the difference that Krashen (1997) makes between language learning and language acquisition. The teacher is explicitly teaching language (learning language) by focusing on pronoun substitutions. The students are *acquiring* language through the read alouds and shared reading experiences. See Chapter 1.

FIGURATIVE LANGUAGE

Ms. Lago knew that she needed to teach figurative language to her children in terms of three elements:

1. The meaning and structure of similes and metaphors; this means helping children to recognize what those two forms of speech are and how they function.

2. The linguistic aspects, that is, the vocabulary aspects of specific similes and metaphors. For example, if children read the following sentence in *Owl Moon*, "I was a shadow as we walked home," they need to understand the meaning of *shadow* so that they can understand the attributes of a shadow.

3. The symbolization of universal truth. In addition, within the Memoir unit of study, she needed to help the children understand that the memoir acts as a metaphor to symbolize a universal truth depicted by the actions and interpretations of the author.

In many of the books she read to the class, similes are more prevalent, but she wanted the children to understand the meaning of metaphors because it is essential to understanding the concept of memoir.

In *Owl Moon*, she saw a great opportunity to teach children about similes. **Similes** are structures that establish a comparison between two unlike things introduced by the word *as* or *like*. Similes always have a predictable structure—*is as*—or *is like*—"*I was as quiet as a dream.*"

She scaffolded the concept of similes:

- She asked children to think about the similes they used regularly in their own lives (Blachowicz & Fisher, 2002). *Jamey is as tall as a giraffe. My desk is as messy as a garbage pail. My father sleeps like a bear.*
- She worked on the common attributes that form the similes from the examples that the children gave her. For example:

Jamey	Giraffe
boy	animal
6th grader	lives in jungle
tall	very tall
likes steak	likes leaves

- She gave the children texts with similes and asked them to find them:
  - Here are some similes they found in *Owl Moon*:

    *Somewhere behind us a train whistle blew, long and low, **like** a sad, sad song.*

    *It was quiet **as** a dream.*

    *. . . the owl pumped its great wings and lifted up the branch **like** a shadow without a sound.*

    *The trees stood still **as** giant statues.*

  - The children found many similes in *The House on Mango Street*. Here are some examples of what they found:

    My Papa's hair is like a broom all up in the air.

    Hair like fur.

    . . . my mother's hair is like little rosettes.

    . . . a house quiet as snow.

    The nose of that Cadillac was pleated like an alligator's.

    [A house] as clean as paper before the poem.

Teaching ***metaphors*** is more difficult. Although they are also figurative comparisons, these are implied or inferred and are not introduced by *like* or *as*. Metaphors are more complicated than similes to understand because the comparison is not made as clear as in the similes. For example, *"I was a shadow as we walked home"* is a metaphor. Metaphors involve implied comparison between two relatively unlike things. Examples include

I was a shadow in the night.

Her teeth are pearls.

Her eyes are stars shining in the sky.

What is difficult about comprehending a metaphor is that the literal interpretation of it will not be enough to understand what the author implies: for example, "I was a shadow." To understand a simile, we have the comparative words (*as, like, than*): for example, "I was as quiet as a shadow."

To teach the concept and structure of metaphors, Ms. Lago used the same strategies she used for similes. She knew that the challenge for her students lay in understanding what was being compared. She scaffolded this process by making explicit the elements that were being compared.

- She asked the children to think about metaphors they used with each other. For example, "Jason is a pig"; "He is a workhorse"; or "My brother is a star."
  a. She discussed the attributes.

My Brother	Star
Boy	Planet
Brilliant	Shines

b. She asked them to identify metaphors in the mentor texts.
c. She worked with the class with the attributes of the metaphors in the mentor texts.

Some of the metaphors from *The House on Mango Street* include:

My hair is lazy. It never obeys barrettes or bands.

My mother's hair is . . . the warm smell of bread before you bake it.

[Until then] I am a red balloon . . . a balloon tied to an anchor.

Finally, to help her students clarify the differences between the two forms of figurative language, she asked children to convert metaphors into similes, as every metaphor can be written as a simile: *I was a shadow—I was as quiet as a shadow.*

Here is an example of how Rosario, who was one of the struggling students in Ms. Lago's class, incorporated the use of figurative language in the first draft of her memoir (see Figure 4.15).

Figure 4.15 Rosario's First Draft

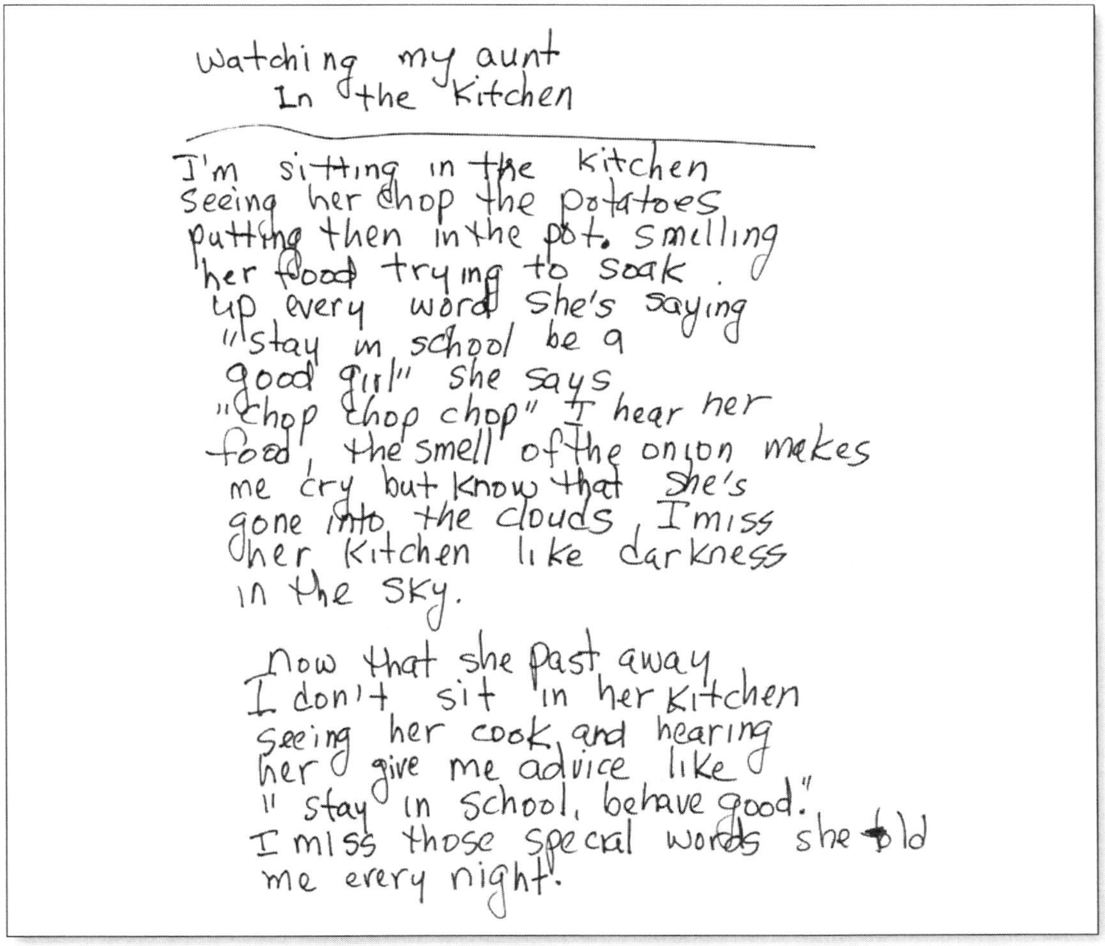

Watching my aunt In the kitchen

I'm sitting in the kitchen seeing her chop the potatoes putting then in the pot. smelling her food trying to soak . up every word she's saying "stay in school be a good girl" she says "chop chop chop" I hear her food, the smell of the onion makes me cry but know that she's gone into the clouds, I miss her kitchen like darkness in the sky.

now that she past away I don't sit in her kitchen seeing her cook, and hearing her give me advice like " stay in school, behave good." I miss those special words she told me every night.

Watching My Aunt in the Kitchen

I'm sitting in the kitchen seeing her chop the potatoes putting them in the pot. smelling her food trying to soak up every word she's saying "[. . .] stay in school, be a good girl" she says "chop chop chop" I hear her food, the smell of the onion makes me cry but know that she's gone into the clouds. I miss her kitchen **like darkness in the sky.**

Now that she past away I don't sit in her kitchen seeing her cook and hearing her give me advise like "stay in school, behave good" I miss those special words she told me every night.

Having a word wall of metaphors and similes (Table 4.16) will create a visual map to help children remember the characteristic of each figure of speech.

Table 4.16   Simile and Metaphor Word Wall

Metaphors: Implied Comparisons Between Two Unlike Things	Similes: Comparisons Between Two Unlike Things Using *like* or *as*
I was a shadow as I walked home.	*I was as quiet as a shadow.*
Her teeth are pearls.	*Her teeth are as white as pearls.*
He was a ghost walking in the night.	*He was like a ghost walking in the night.*

To get her students to think more deeply about the genre, Ms. Lago put up a chart (Figure 4.17), which she filled out with the help of the children, analyzing the craft the authors used in some of the mentor texts she had read.

CONCLUSION

In this chapter, we have integrated some of the concepts that the Memoir Unit of Study entails, with the language structures that are necessary for the children to learn in order to develop a full understanding of the unit. Read aloud and shared reading are key structures that we can use to motivate and foster understanding of what this genre is all about. We explore how open-ended and specific questions can trigger thinking skills that not only develop language but also in-depth thinking processes. In addition, the chapter describes different language structures that the mentor texts present and that we can reinforce, once the books have been read and understood. In this way, language, vocabulary, and syntax as well as figurative language are taught in context.

Figure 4.17   Ms. Lago's Chart

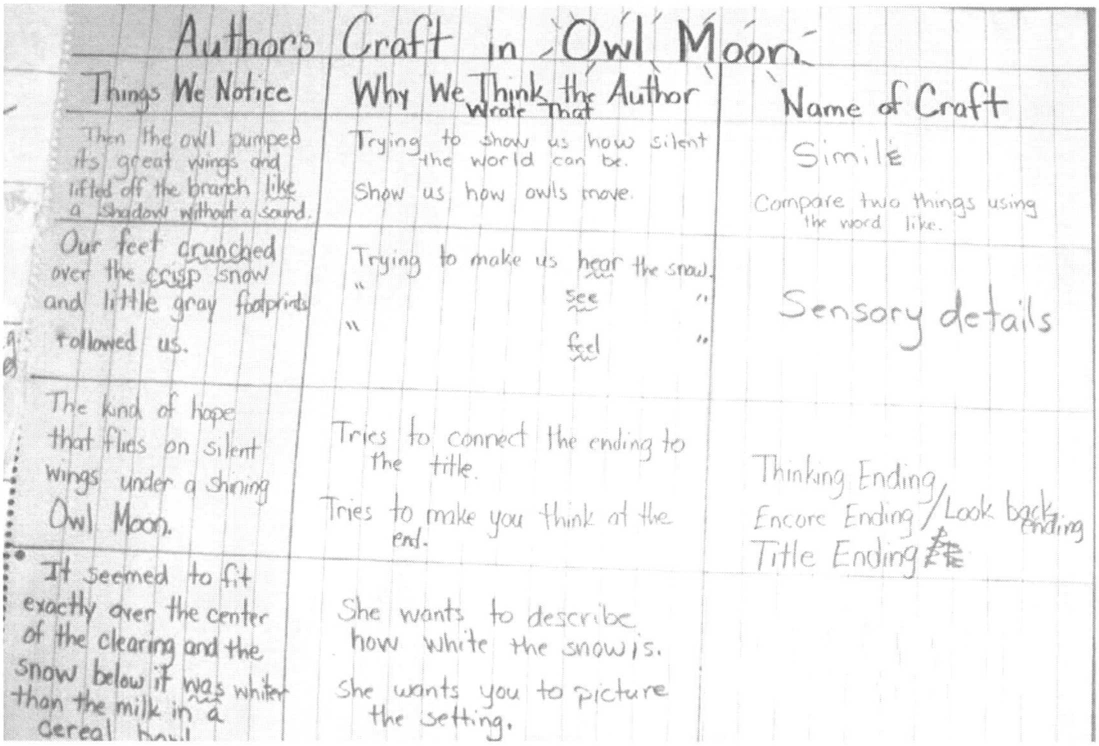

From Soledad Lago.

TEACHER SELF-ASSESSMENT FOR THE UNIT

Have I . . .	
Created a Memoir planning chart integrating language and concept goals?	
Informed students at the beginning of the unit about what they are going to be learning? (Overview)	
Made a chart illuminating the characteristics of the Memoir genre, adding to it as we read different memoirs?	
Looked at the mentor texts I will use in order to find challenging vocabulary that may present problems for the students?	

Used scaffolding strategies to model academic language? That is, introducing Tier 2 and 3 words based on Tier 1 words (*reflect—to think*)?	
Used graphic organizers (KWL charts) to trigger background knowledge, or to help students understand difficult concepts without heavy language load?	
Provided frequent and explicit feedback to the students?	
Developed rubrics tailored to this unit so that students can self-assess?	
Created enough opportunities for children to work collaboratively and have time to discuss and share ideas?	
Given enough language support to early stage EL students? Are they in three-way partnerships? Conferences? Peer work?	
Created thinking prompts that reflect the requirements of the unit, e.g., "The thought I have about this is . . ."?	
Developed a student assessment chart?	

5

Social Studies Unit

Colonial Times and the American Revolution (Grade 4)

THE ENGLISH LANGUAGE LEARNER AND THE SOCIAL STUDIES CURRICULUM

One of the biggest challenges that we face when we teach content area curriculum to EL and struggling children is our need to make the subject matter accessible to the students without simplifying the material. This is not an easy task because each subject area has specific, specialized vocabulary and terminology that the students need to understand in order to integrate the concepts they need to learn. This observation is particularly appropriate when we are teaching social studies, since we also have to develop background knowledge about American history and institutions that many ELs do not have.

As EL children move up in the grades, the social studies curriculum carries with it increasing *cognitive demands* (the understanding of concepts difficult to comprehend), and it requires the knowledge of *technical* (Tier 3) vocabulary specifically relevant to this subject area, for example, *slavery*, *freedom*, *civilization*, *culture*, *taxation*, and *independence*. Deborah Short (1996) writes that to do well in social studies, students need to have literacy skills, and those skills include reading, writing, speaking, researching, and organizing information in English. Chall (1983) states that using social studies texts is the best way of exercising reading comprehension, since students have to learn new information and integrate it with what they already know. The challenge for teachers is to find strategies that are going to reduce the cognitive load without watering down the content (Szpara & Ahmad, 2006).

In this chapter, we aim to

- supply you with a myriad of **activities** you can plan in order to develop the background knowledge and language skills that EL children need in order to fully participate in the social studies curriculum that is being taught in their classroom and
- guide you **step-by-step** through these activities.

You should choose the activities that will work best for your specific population.

Although both of us work in a variety of classrooms, we focus in this chapter on our experiences in Rachel Bard's fourth-grade classroom in a public school in New York City. Most of Rachel's students are long-term English language learners from Spanish-speaking backgrounds, with low literacy skills in both languages. Rachel's class encapsulates many of the issues that ELs face as they try to meet social studies standards in the upper elementary grades. In our initial discussion about our collaboration, Rachel stated that one of her major concerns about teaching social studies to her students is their lack of background knowledge and inference skills. Rachel said, *"A big challenge in my class is getting students to draw a conclusion that combines information they already have with new information they are learning from books and from discussions."*

Major Challenges in Planning the Unit

- Building *background knowledge*: How can we get kids to relate to this topic? (Does the topic remind them of any other? Do they have experience with this? Do they have knowledge about this subject?)
- Making the *content and the concepts* accessible to ELs: developing strategies to help reduce cognitive load
- Developing the *academic and technical vocabulary* children need in order to understand the concepts
- Teaching children *how to find information and organize their new ideas*
- Teaching children *how to record and present what they have learned*
- Developing the *critical thinking skills* needed for this unit (collecting, sorting out, analyzing, interpreting, and synthesizing information; understanding cause-and-effect relationships)

Planning the Unit

This sample unit is part of the social studies curriculum in fourth grade in New York State. The curriculum connects local (NYS) history with the rest of early American history, including the Colonial and Revolutionary periods, the beginning of the new nation, and industrial growth and expansion. For our work in Rachel's class, we focused on the Colonial and Revolutionary periods, using audiovisual equipment, read alouds, shared reading, and shared writing as our main tools to develop background knowledge, concepts, and language skills.

Table 5.1 includes content and language objectives. Also see the Planning Chart: Scaffolding Content and Language Goals (Social Studies) at http://www.corwin.com/connectingcontent4ell.

Table 5.1 Planning Template for the Colonial and Revolutionary Periods

Audiovisuals and Class Trips	Read Aloud	Critical Thinking Skills	Shared Reading and Shared Writing	Language Skills That the Unit Requires
Videos				
Developing background knowledge: • Does this topic remind me of any other? • Class discussions • Graphic organizers to help students take notes • KWL charts	Critical thinking skills during interactive read aloud: • Think alouds • Thinking prompts • Turn and talk • Partner work • Note taking • Write main ideas on sticky notes and retell them	A—Identifying cause and effect B—Analyzing C—Comparing D—Inferring E—Synthesizing F—Interpreting G—Explaining H—Summarizing I—Categorizing	Use shared reading to teach children strategies for reading nonfiction. Show: • Skim and scan, meaning of titles and subtitles, look for key words, etc. • Shared reading to work on syntax and vocabulary • Dealing with "tricky" words	• Syntactic structures • Past tense • Cause and effect connectives: **because, so, consequently, therefore, due to the fact, since, as a result, the reason for** • Relative clauses: The colonists **that** came from England wanted religious freedom • Sequential markers in time: **then, following, before, in the end**
Photographs and Other Visual Aids	Books I Will Use	Thinking Prompts	Shared Reading Texts	Technical Words (Tier 3)
• Illustrations depicting life for the settlers and for the Iroquois: houses, dress styles, differences in environment	• *Colonial Life* • *The Thirteen Colonies* • *Liberty!* • *The Revolutionary War*	A—What caused ___? What is another possible cause of ___? B—What would happen if . . .? C—How is ___ like ___? How are ___ and ___ different? D—Predict what will happen if ___. E—What is your conclusion? F—I What generalization can you make from this information? G—Give an example of ___.	• National Geographic for Kids: "First Thanksgiving" • "If you lived in Colonial Times" (chapters) • "If you were there when they signed the Declaration of Independence"	(These are specific to this unit.) **Examples** • Culture • Revolution • Slavery • Colonies • Geography • Taxation • Freedom, etc. . . .
Class Trips	Word Wall	Small-Group Work	Shared Writing	Academic Words (Tier 2)
• Natural History Museum • NY Historical Society	• Word sorts on word wall with key words and synonyms	• Concept definition maps, student reports • Create a mural and label it	• Class trips • Synthesize information and integrate new concepts • Show students how to organize information	(These you use across the curriculum.) **Examples** • Cite, define, identify, label • Describe, diagram, compare, evidence, etc.
	Individual Dictionaries			
	• Children compile their own dictionary for this unit			

Theory-to-Practice Connection

This planning chart takes into account the need to develop background knowledge about the content of the unit, as well as the thinking skills and technical vocabulary (Tier 3 words) that the students need in order to process the information. See Chapter 1.

CONCEPTS AND TEACHING TOOLS

The first step of our planning was to identify the key concepts the students were expected to learn and find ways to present the information with comprehensible language without watering down concepts. To do this, we provided the students with visual and written information to support their learning. In Table 5.2, there are several ideas that helped us plan the unit, incorporating different teaching tools. Also see the Planning Chart: Social Studies Concepts and Teaching Tools at http://www.corwin.com/connectingcontent4ell.

Table 5.2 Concepts and Teaching Tools

Concepts	How Do I Teach Them?	How Do I Make Sure Students Understand?
The colonists came to America for a variety of reasons.	• Videos • Read aloud • Class discussion: activate background knowledge	• KWL charts • Video charts • Small group work
• The role of geography in the establishment of the colonies • The Pilgrims • Different characteristics of the colonies • Life in the New York colony	• Read aloud: colonial life, the thirteen colonies, etc. • Map to help students locate colonies • Shared reading to help children read different sources of info • Interactive cognate word wall to improve comprehension (Spanish speaking students) • Unit word wall	• Concept definition map about colonial period • Work with historical sources in groups • Add their initial to word wall every time they use new word
Difference in historical times—how life was then and how it is now • How was life during the British colonies?	• Visuals (pictures, drawings) • Videos • Read aloud: If you lived in Colonial Times . . . • Trip to Historical Society	• KWL chart before read aloud: Have students work in groups to research what they want to know about life in Colonial America. Students take notes during reading.
Taxation without representation • What made the Americans rebel against the British?	• Class discussion	• Cause-and-effect graphic organizer • Group work

Concepts	How Do I Teach Them?	How Do I Make Sure Students Understand?
Impact of the War in NYS and NYC • How did the American Revolution affect the lives of people in New York?	• Video: PBS: *Colonial House*	• Timeline of steps toward the Revolutionary War will help children visualize and process concept definition map • Concept definition map about the American Revolution
The Declaration of Independence • The issue of slavery • The signing of the Constitution	• Read aloud: If you were there when they signed the Constitution . . . • Shared reading: Read slave poems	• Activity: Children create a classroom set of rights and obligations

BREAKING THE PLAN INTO DOABLE PARTS

Assessing and Developing Background Knowledge

Overview: Getting children to relate to this topic

Rachel started the social studies unit on the Colonial Period and the Revolutionary War by asking the students how many of them were born outside of the United States. Several children raised their hands, and she asked them how they had traveled to this country. Some children said they had flown, others said they had come by car or bus, and one child said he had come by boat to Florida. The students then brainstormed about feelings and thoughts associated with their trip to this new land. As children began to speak, she wrote what they said on a chart: "flew in a plane with my mother," "rode in a bus," "traveled by car," "left my family in Mexico," "was scared at night," "felt sad," "did not know anybody," "felt strange." The teacher then told the class that they now were going to explore how the pioneers traveled to America, how they felt when they reached this new land, and how they adjusted to it. She introduced a few new terms: *colony, settlement, pilgrims,* and *religious freedom*. Then, she showed the class a short video about the first colonies. After the video, Rachel led a class discussion connecting the experiences of the children with the experiences of the pilgrims. In this way, she established a bridge between the children's experiences and the new information she was introducing.

Through the use of visuals and audiovisuals, Rachel helped students envision life during the Colonial and Revolutionary periods. She used:

- Photos
- Illustrations
- Videos
- Graphs
- Letters
- Diary entries

- Newspapers
- Maps
- Class trips
- Visits to historical societies

She felt that the more visuals were used, the easier it would be for the students to grasp concepts without an overload of language.

Visuals and audiovisuals

Videos

We planned carefully how Rachel was going to introduce and show the video *Colonial House* (PBS Home Video, 2004). This video portrays modern-day people living in the same conditions as the first settlers. For each segment she planned to use, we asked ourselves the following questions:

- What do we want the children to focus on?
- What is our purpose in showing this video?
- What is the vocabulary that the children will need to interpret this source of information?

Rachel showed only small segments with a specific purpose in mind. Here are the steps that she followed:

1. *Introduction to the video:* She summarized what portion she wanted the children to focus on, that is, "Today we are going to look at how people gathered food during early Colonial times."

2. *Purpose of showing the video:* She explicitly told the children what she wanted them to do: "We are going to see how gathering food affected the daily lives of the colonists."

3. *Categorizing information:* She provided categories for the students to organize their information:
   - Family relationships
   - Daily chores
   - Housing, etc.

4. *Use of selected scenes:* She showed segments of the video several times and then held a whole-class conversation after the video. The Note Taking Organizer for Video is also available at http://www.corwin.com/connectingcontent4ell.

5. *Group work:* Students were divided into small groups to fill in a chart focusing on a specific aspect of the video (Table 5.3). For example, one group of students can focus on shelter, another group can focus on food, and so forth.

6. *Class discussion:* Before Ms. Bard showed the video, she provided students with a graphic organizer (Table 5.3) to structure their thinking. The last column pushes the students to make an inference.

Table 5.3   Note-Taking Organizer for Colonial Period Video

Category of Information	I Noticed . . .	This Means . . .
Shelter		
Daily chores		
Food		

Copyright © 2011 by Corwin. All rights reserved. Reprinted from *Connecting Content and Academic Language for English Learners and Struggling Students, Grades 2–6*, by Ruth Swinney and Patricia Velasco. Thousand Oaks, CA: Corwin, www.corwin.com. Reproduction authorized only for the local school site or nonprofit organization that has purchased this book.

Theory-to-Practice Connection

The use of graphic organizers helps store new information and allows students to remember key information without language overload. See Chapter 1.

Pictures and illustrations

Another way in which Rachel encouraged the children to visualize life during the Colonial and Revolutionary periods was through the use of illustrations. She wanted the students to compare the life of the Iroquois in New York State before the colonization with the life of the Dutch as they settled in the area.

To do this, she showed two illustrations side by side to the students and asked, *"Can you tell me what is different in these two illustrations?"* One illustration showed a beautiful landscape depicting Iroquois men, women, and children going about their chores: tending to their animals, planting, cooking, and hunting. The other illustration showed a Dutch settlement with lots of houses, no trees or foliage visible. She walked the students through the process of analyzing the visuals and making inferences about what life was before the settlers came to America, and how life was after they settled in NY state by comparing and contrasting the two illustrations.

Joana	(Pointing to the picture of the landscape and the Iroquois:) It looks peaceful; they took care of the land.
Teacher	I am so proud of you! You are using what you already know! But I want you to tell me first only what you see.
Joana	I see a group of native . . . of Iroquois in a small group of . . . it is peaceful and nice trees and mountains.
Chris	(Pointing to the illustration of the Dutch settlement:) In this picture it looks as if there were many people living in that town, they needed to build all those houses. (Pointing to the picture of the landscape and the Iroquois:) In this picture there were very few people, they did not need to cut trees. The Dutch needed to cut a lot of trees to build all those houses.
Brian	That means that many more people came to settle, comparing to the Indians . . . I mean Iroquois.

Rachel then wrote the students' observations on a T chart (Figure 5.4). She divided the chart in two parts: "I noticed" and "This tells me." This was another step in her effort to build inference skills in her students.

Figure 5.4 Ms. Bard Writes What the Students Say on the Chart

Figure 5.5   Closer View of the Chart With Some of the Students' Comments

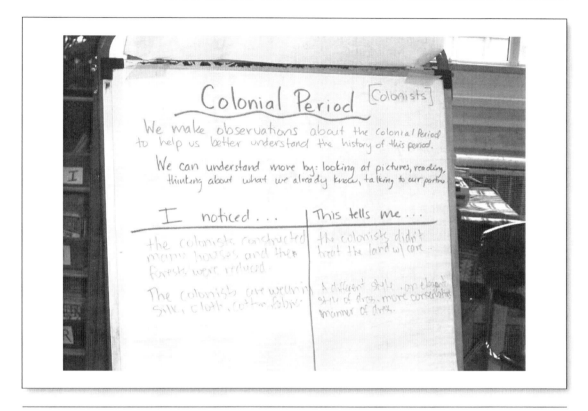

From Rachel Bard.

The children copied the chart in their notebooks, as they knew they would have to use it later for their independent work.

Rachel showed two more illustrations depicting the Iroquois and the settlers and then asked the children to describe what the different mode of dress said about the culture of both groups.

Ms. Bard	Turn to your partner and describe what you notice about the way the clothes were different.

After the children discussed what they observed with their partners, the teacher (who was listening to their conversations) highlighted some of their comments and wrote them on the chart.

Teacher	I heard Joana say that the Iroquois wore animal furs, and they did not wear a lot of clothes. The Europeans wore long skirts and hats. What does this tell us about their lives?
Brian	It tells us that the Europeans were more . . . strict?
Diosmary	They (Iroquois) did not have cloth. The Europeans had silk . . . cotton.
Teacher	Those are great observations. You noticed that the Iroquois used furs, and that made you think they did not have materials to make clothes. Also you noticed they were different cultures.

Rachel organized the students into small groups and told them, "You will now go back to your tables. On each table, there is a pile of books with illustrations of colonial life. On your chart, you will copy what you noticed, and then what that observation tells you." After working in their small groups for 15 minutes, the students returned to the meeting area and shared their findings.

The teacher used photographs and illustrations to help her students visualize key concepts that she wanted them to learn. She knew that using illustrations can help students make inferences and visualize the historical moment that the photographs and illustrations represent. This prepares the students for the use of primary documents, which is part of the social studies curriculum.

To support comprehension and inference skills, we adapted a worksheet designed and developed by the Education Staff, National Archives and Records Administration (http://www.archives.gov/education/lessons/worksheets/photo.html) (see Table 5.6). It helps students to organize the process of examining a photograph or an illustration, and it focuses their observational skills. For a full-sized printable version of the Photo Analysis Worksheet, see http://www.corwin.com/connectingcontent4ell.

Table 5.6 Photo Analysis Worksheet

Step 1. Observation (What are we noticing?)		
Look at the photograph or illustration—What do you notice? Divide the photograph/illustration in 4 parts. Look at every section. Think about the details in each section.		
List the people, objects, activities you observed in the photograph/illustration.		
People	**Objects**	**Activities**
Step 2. Inference (This makes me think . . . I can guess that. . . .)		
Based on what you have observed above, list three things this photograph/illustration tells you.		
People	**Objects**	**Activities**
Step 3. Questions		
What questions do you have about this photograph/illustration? How could you find answers to your questions?		
People	**Objects**	**Activities**

Copyright © 2011 by Corwin. All rights reserved. Reprinted from *Connecting Content and Academic Language for English Learners and Struggling Students, Grades 2–6,* by Ruth Swinney and Patricia Velasco. Thousand Oaks, CA: Corwin, www.corwin.com. Reproduction authorized only for the local school site or nonprofit organization that has purchased this book.

ANCHORING THE UNIT IN A READ ALOUD

Interactive read aloud provided a perfect opportunity for anchoring this unit; it helped to expand the students' background knowledge and teach new concepts and vocabulary that the students could not access on their own. Rachel Bard saw this as an opportunity to scaffold and bridge for the students by providing contextual clues. During the read aloud, she provided opportunities for partner talk and whole-class conversations. This helped the students clarify their ideas and integrate new information.

As she read aloud, the teacher modeled for her students the ways in which they should read nonfiction in order to access information. She introduced the read aloud activity by *previewing* the text and telling children what she expected of them, setting a purpose for her reading (i.e., gathering information and understanding how life was during colonial times) and making clear the strategy that she was going to model (i.e., we are going to stop and think about what we are reading and ask questions when we don't understand).

Table 5.7 shows the read aloud plan we made with Rachel. We incorporated activities that not only helped students develop vocabulary but also used strategies to model critical thinking skills. This plan was implemented over several days.

Table 5.7 Template for Read Aloud: Life in a New Land

Prior to the Read Aloud	During the Read Aloud	After the Read Aloud
• Describe the strategy you will use, e.g., "We are going to stop and think about what we read and retell our partners." • A summary generally integrates the elements of the chapter. We tell children what to listen for: Today we learn about the three main groups of colonists that came to North America. One group settled in Jamestown, Virginia. The other two groups, the Puritans and the Quakers, wanted religious freedom. First they all wanted a life like they had in their homeland but after a while they adapted to the new land and traded with the Indians.	Think alouds: During the read aloud the teacher will model the sort of thinking a good reader is apt to do as he or she reads. Think alouds: • I wonder why "they changed the way they made their homes." • This makes me think that there was a lot of communication with the Indians. • Close your eyes and make a movie in your mind about how the day may have gone for the colonists.	Focused partner and whole-group conversations that deepen comprehension of the text: • What do we know about the way a colonist lived? • Do you think that a colonist's life was an easy or hard one? And why do you think that? • In the text it says, "After one hundred years, Indian culture and life on the east coast of North America had nearly disappeared." Why do you think that happened? Use higher level questions: • *Synthesis*: "What would happen if …." • *Evaluation*: "Tell your partner what you think about …." • *Knowledge*: "What happened after …." • *Analysis*: "Turn and tell your partner how the colonists would have survived if … happened."

(Continued)

Table 5.7 (Continued)

Prior to the Read Aloud	During the Read Aloud	After the Read Aloud
Choose 3–5 key words to teach on any one day, and choose vocabulary that is important in order to understand concepts, e.g., colony, settlement, homesick, searching, scarce Describe, use pictures when possible, use synonyms, explanations on the run	When the language of the text is particularly challenging, add synonyms to clarify the meaning of words, e.g., "Settlement, that means little town."	Recall the text using the initial 3–5 words. Reread the text or revisit it, this time perhaps teaching a few more vocabulary words. Again, 3–5 words, using methods described earlier.
	Rearrange syntax to clarify, inserting a noun in place of an indefinite pronoun. Instead of "they," say, "the colonists."	
You may use very brief partner work to invite kids to "try on" the new words. They can describe the new terms using their own words.	Three-way partnerships so less fluent students can immerse themselves in language models. Turn and talk—focus on comprehension and synthesis: Why did the colonists want everything the way it was in England?	Partner work using vocabulary words: word sorts, concept definition charts, words in context

Theory-to-Practice Connection

Through the use of interactive read aloud the teacher was able to create a context for this unit; through this structure she expanded the students' background knowledge and taught new concepts and vocabulary that the students were not able to access on their own. See Chapter 3.

To anchor this unit, Rachel used the collection of *True Books About American History* published by Scholastic. These books describe life in colonial times, the Declaration of Independence, the Revolutionary War, and the issues of the 13 colonies in great detail. The books also have illustrations that make it easy for children to understand the content and develop background knowledge about the period. Although they are picture books, they have vocabulary and concepts that are difficult for ELs to read on their own. In this classroom, we used them in read aloud and also in shared reading, and at the same time, the children were able to read them independently after they heard the text in read aloud. We also used many other picture books; they are listed in the references.

Although Rachel read many books on the subject to her fourth graders, here we use a **segment** from *Colonial Life* by Brendan January (2000) to show how she scaffolded the concepts for her students through read aloud, and how she developed critical thinking skills through the activities she organized around each chapter. Rachael read the whole book to her class.

Chapter 1 of *Colonial Life* (January, 2000)

Life in a New Land

In 1607, a ship filled with people from England landed on the coast of the land we now call Virginia. With the permission of King James I of England, they had set to start a new life in a new land.

With axes and spades they cleared a spot in the forest. They built a tiny village of mud huts.

This village became Jamestown—the first successful English settlement, or colony, in North America. Named after King James I, this new village was a colony belonging to England; the people who lived there were called colonists.

Before the Read Aloud

Before the read aloud, Rachel did a picture or chapter walk to guide students to ask themselves whether they had any ideas about this subject. She provided time for students to brainstorm before filling out the first part of the chart below (see Table 5.8). She was helping students access prior knowledge by helping them interact with the text before she read it to them. The teacher set up the stage for how children were going to listen: "*We are going to read a chapter about the early settlements, but more than that, this chapter is about how the settlers adjusted to their new lives.*"

The teacher provided a graphic organizer for her students to write their notes on before and after the read aloud.

Table 5.8 Student Graphic Organizer for the Read Aloud

My Ideas Before the Reading	My Ideas After the Reading: What Did I Learn?

Copyright © 2011 by Corwin. All rights reserved. Reprinted from *Connecting Content and Academic Language for English Learners and Struggling Students, Grades 2–6*, by Ruth Swinney and Patricia Velasco. Thousand Oaks, CA: Corwin, www.corwin.com. Reproduction authorized only for the local school site or nonprofit organization that has purchased this book.

During the Read Aloud

As Rachel read the text, these are the scaffolds that she provided for her students during read aloud:

Scaffolds Rachel Used During Read Aloud

- Explanations on the run: "The Jamestown colonists eagerly—that means *excitedly*."
- Rearranging syntax so that kids can understand sophisticated texts. Instead of "This village became Jamestown—the first successful English settlement or colony in North America," she said, "Jamestown became the first successful English settlement or colony in North America."
- Think alouds: "I wonder why they built mud huts."
- Introducing new vocabulary in context: "There are several new words here; let's see if we can predict what they mean from our reading."

During the read aloud, Rachel focused the thinking of the students by posing guiding questions to clarify the main idea before she read key paragraphs. As students turned and talked to their partners, they focused on the guiding questions. For example:

- How was Jamestown founded?
- What made the colonists settle in different places?

Skills That Rachel Developed During Read Aloud

During read aloud the teacher focused on developing critical thinking skills through think alouds and partner work.

Think Alouds

- Analyzing: "I wonder what caused—" "What could be another reason for . . . ."
- Comparing: "In what ways was their life in the colonies like it was in Europe?"
- Explaining: "Let's look for examples of how the colonists farmed."
- Summarizing: "Let's think about what we learned today."
- Envisioning: "I am picturing how the settlers and the colonists talked to each other."

Partner Work

- Explaining: "Turn to your partner and tell him what you are thinking."
- Compare and contrast. "Give your partner an example of how life was different from. . . ."
- Inferring: "Tell your partner why you think the colonists had to emigrate from Europe."
- Synthesizing information: "Tell your partner what you learned in this chapter."
- Retelling: "Turn to your partner and tell him what we have read up to now."

After the Read Aloud

Rachel wanted her students to be able to retell what she had read, but she noticed that they were having a hard time retelling. They often missed parts of the text. To help students organize information, she scaffolded the process of summarizing using the retelling graphic organizer (Table 5.9). The Retelling Graphic Organizer is also available at http://www.corwin.com/connectingcontent4ell.

Table 5.9   Retelling Graphic Organizer

Beginning	Middle	End	Sequencing Words
First the settlers landed in Jamestown	Then the pilgrims landed in Plymouth	The colonists built Jamestown	first next then second third while last after finally

Sequencing words indicate the logical connections among sentences and paragraphs. The students worked in small groups. After they finished filling up the organizer, she had them practice doing the retelling with each other.

THINKING SKILLS USED THROUGHOUT THE UNIT: LANGUAGE PROMPTS

Throughout the unit, Rachel was consistent with the questions that she posed to her students. Notice that she made a point of asking questions that made her students interpret or infer information, since this was one of her main objectives. She also gave language prompts or sentence starters that covered a variety of thinking processes. These questions and language prompts (see Table 5.10) were used in small-group work, whole-group discussions, and partner talk.

Theory-to-Practice Connection

Here the teacher structures questions that elicit high-order thinking skills: synthesizing, comparing and contrasting, and inferring. See Chapter 2.

Table 5.10	Questions and Language Prompts

Questions the Teacher Used	Language Prompts or Sentence Starters for the Students
Compare and Contrast	*Connecting New and Old Information*
• *What do you think about the relationship between ... and ...?*	• *This reminds me of....* • *I know about this topic because I....*
Inference	**Questioning Prompts**
• *What are your ideas about ...?* • *What is this passage really about?* • *What is this chapter saying?* • *What are your views about ...?* • *What would have happened if ...?*	• *I wonder why....* • *What does this word mean?* • *I have a question about....*
	Making Inferences
	• *I think this means....* • *I think the book is telling us....*
	Synthesis
	• *This passage is really about....* • *My opinion of _____ is....* • *The most important ideas are....* • *I think that learning about the colonial period is important because....*

VOCABULARY DEVELOPMENT

As the unit progressed, we noticed that many children had a hard time understanding some of the technical vocabulary in the texts and during read aloud. Some of the activities that Rachel used to deepen word knowledge include **shades of meaning, use of cognates, word sorts,** and **concept definition maps.**

Shades of Meaning

We felt that teaching one word alone would not give the students sufficient understanding of the concept behind the word. Rachel used a **shades of meaning** chart (see Figure 5.11). She started with the word *revolution*, as in our example here, and moved on to the different shades of the meaning of that word, eliciting the words from the children by brainstorming.

As an added activity, to help students contextualize the concepts, students were asked to work in groups to develop a timeline for the event used in the shades of meaning activity. We gave students index cards naming the important steps to the event, or pictures depicting important scenes, and asked them to arrange them in order. Students took turns in presenting their timelines. Other students in the group asked questions such as:

- Why is this particular event important?
- How did this event contribute to the American Revolution/settlement of the different colonies?

| **Figure 5.11** | Shades of Meaning for the Word *Revolution* |

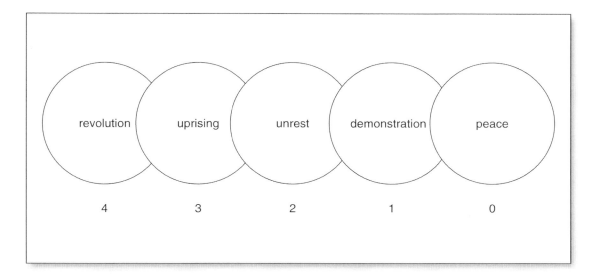

During this activity, the teacher provided signal words for sequencing, which is an important skill for EL students in social studies:

- First
- Second
- Then
- Next
- After
- Finally

Use of Cognates

This unit presented a great opportunity for the use of ***cognates*** to help the students in this class, since they all came from Spanish-speaking backgrounds, as there are many common words between the two languages, for example, *revolution/revolución*, *soldier/soldado*, *bayonet/bayoneta*, *resistance/resistencia*, and *government/gobierno*. We suggest a word wall with cognates.

Word Sorts

Another way in which Rachel helped her students relate the words to concepts was though using ***word sorts***. In this case, she gave her students the categories and had them work in small groups to classify the words (see Figure 5.12).

Concept Definition Maps

Rachel asked her students to work in groups to use the information they had gathered during the read alouds and independent reading. She used the format of a ***concept definition***

Figure 5.12 Word Sorts for Colonial America

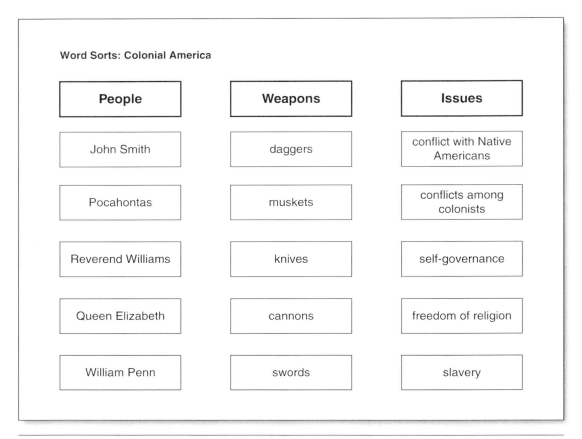

Source: Based on Echevarria, Vogt, and Short (2000).

map to help them synthesize the information they had learned about the Colonial as well as the Revolutionary periods. Figure 5.13 is an example of the latter.

Theory-to-Practice Connection

Mastering the vocabulary of the unit and connecting the words to the concepts they represent requires multiple exposures though different activities. See Chapter 1.

SHARED READING: WORKING WITH LANGUAGE GOALS

Rachel Bard used shared reading to work on the language goals she had for this unit. As always during shared reading, students followed along as the teacher read; they chimed in along with the teacher or read at designated times. Students had their own copies in small

Figure 5.13 Concept Definition Map: American Revolution

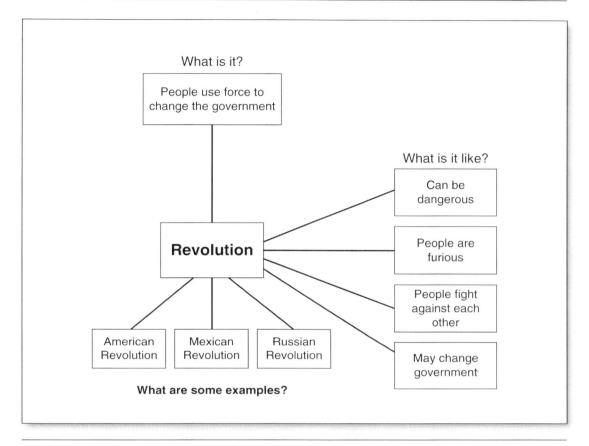

Source: Based on Echeverria, Vogt, and Short (2000).

booklets, so they were able to work with their partners later practicing the strategies they had learned. The following are examples of different strategies used in this classroom in the course of several days. Each activity did not take more than 15 minutes, and sometimes the teacher worked with the whole class while at other times she divided them into small groups.

The following examples are taken from *If You Were There When They Signed the Constitution* by Elizabeth Levy (1987). This book is part of a series that helps children understand important times in American history. It describes the Constitution of the United States, the reasons for the Revolutionary War, and the Declaration of Independence. Many of the students in this class had a hard time reading this book on their own. Reading key portions of the book during shared reading helped the EL students develop the information they needed.

Developing Strategies for Reading Nonfiction

Understanding cause and effect and the signal words (conjunctions) that are used in these structures

In social studies texts, cause-and-effect structures are very common. Using graphic organizers, Rachel helped her students understand the different structures used in expository texts. Here is an example of one of the shared reading activities she used; she asked the students to fill in the information in the chart:

In 1763 King George III demanded more and more taxes from the American colonies. The colonists didn't like having to pay a tax on everything–on paper, glass, and tea. **But** the colonists had no one to speak for them in the English parliament. "No taxation without representation!" they cried.

After a while many Americans wanted to rebel, to break away from England and become independent.

Source: Based on *If You Were There When They Signed the Constitution* (Levy, 1987, p. 8).

Then she used a graphic organizer (Table 5.14) to help her students understand the structure. The Cause-and-Effect Graphic Organizer is also available at http://www.corwin.com/connectingcontent4ell.)

Table 5.14 Cause-and-Effect Graphic Organizer

Cause	Signal Words	Effect
In 1763 King George demanded more taxes from the American Colonies	for this reason that is why therefore as a result so	the colonists rebelled

In cause-and-effect constructions, the cause usually comes first followed by the effect. However, this is not applicable when we work with *because*, where the effect comes before the cause (see Table 5.15).

Table 5.15 Cause-and-Effect (Because) Graphic Organizer

Effect	Signal Word	Cause
The colonists rebelled	because	in 1763 King George began to demand more taxes from the American colonies

There was a chart in the class with the following signal words for cause and effect:

- for this reason
- thus
- in order to
- as a result
- because
- consequently
- so that
- on account of
- therefore
- accordingly

Syntax and Elements of Cohesion

Social studies texts present particular challenges for EL students because they use relative clauses, irregular past tenses, and pronouns. These patterns make the content difficult to understand. To show children how to understand these structures, Rachel used read aloud texts in shared reading, since the children already knew the content and were free to focus on the syntax. The goal was to develop strategies for children to understand these patterns, so that they could process these sentence structures when they read independently.

Relative clauses

Relative clauses are often confusing for ELs because they have a main and a subordinate idea, and children have a hard time figuring out the meaning. Relative clauses have two sentences. The second one (or subordinate clause) is introduced by *that*, *who*, or *which*, and many readers do not know what this word means in the sentence. Here are some examples of relative clauses:

> *King George III was the king who raised taxes for the American colonies.*
>
> *The Pilgrims belonged to a religious group that wanted freedom to practice.*
>
> *The Battle of Lexington was one of the first battles which started the American Revolution.*

For a more detailed description of these types of sentences, read Chapter 1.

Working in small groups, Rachel did a strategy lesson to model how to process relative clauses. This experience gave the students an opportunity to practice with the teacher the strategy and then do it independently.

Modeling

Rachel told the students that a good strategy for recognizing a relative clause is that they are often introduced by *who* or *that*. She presented the following paragraph and she said, as if asking herself, "Here is a relative clause and I know because it has '*that*.'" She underlined it (bold letters in the text).

> *The colonists began to eat products **that** grew in this part of the world.*

The next part of the strategy was to break this sentence into two. Rachel explained that there is a sentence before *that* and one that comes after.

The last part of the process is identifying what *that* stands for. Rachel connected products with an arrow to *that*:

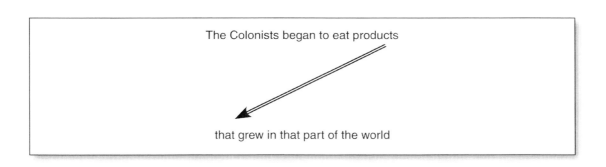

Rachel's final step in this strategy was to emphasize that *that* is referring to *products*.

Active engagement or joined practice between teacher and students

The next step was to start practicing together with the students. Rachel had another relative clause written on the chart paper:

> *They built new homes that took advantage of the region's weather. Slowly, the colonists created a new way of living.*

Rachel reminded the students of the steps and walked the students through them again. The students came up with the following two sentences:

> *They built new homes that took advantage of the region's weather.*

1. They built new homes

2. that (referring to *the homes*) took advantage of the region's weather.

The final part of this **strategy lesson** was a reminder of the steps that can help recognize and process a relative clause. Rachel summarized it as follows:

> *Remember that we recognize a relative clause by the "that," "who," or "which." These sentences have two parts, before and after the "that, who, or which," and we have to find what "that, who, or which" is substituting for.*

Finally, the students were sent to their tables, where they were asked to find in their texts one relative clause and to practice processing it.

Pronouns and substitutions

Pronouns are ways of linking paragraphs (for a more detailed description, read Chapter 1). In Figure 5.16, Rachel used arrows to connect the pronouns.

In a subsequent lesson, Rachel focused on substitutions by asking her students guiding questions as she read. She used the same text:

> *In 1607 a ship filled with people from England landed on the coast of the land we now call Virginia. With permission of King James I of England, they had to start life in a new land.* (From January, 2000)

Rachel asked, "New land is referring to . . . ?" (Pointing to Virginia and drawing an arrow):

> *With axes and spades they cleared a spot in the forest . They built a tiny village of mud huts. This village became Jamestown—the first successful English settlement in North America.* (From January, 2000)

Rachel asked, "The first English settlement in North America is referring to . . . ?"
This time the students answered: "Jamestown." Rachel drew an arrow connecting Jamestown to *first successful English settlement*. As with the previous exercise, Rachel asked

Figure 5.16 Pronouns and Substitutions Exercise

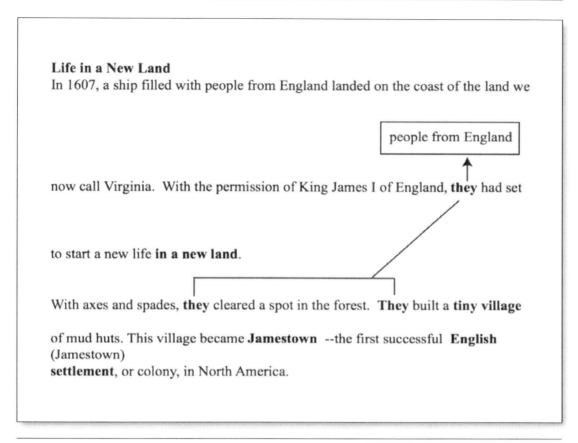

Life in a New Land
In 1607, a ship filled with people from England landed on the coast of the land we

people from England

now call Virginia. With the permission of King James I of England, **they** had set

to start a new life **in a new land**.

With axes and spades, **they** cleared a spot in the forest. **They** built a **tiny village**

of mud huts. This village became **Jamestown** --the first successful **English**
(Jamestown)
settlement, or colony, in North America.

Source: Based on *Colonial Life* (January, 2000).

the students to practice recognizing substitutions. She recommended that they could use their finger to point to the specific substitutions that they found.

Verbs

In this unit, we use verbs in the past tense, and these can have irregular forms. We used this shared reading exercise to practice the correct tenses. We asked the students to say the correct form of the verb as we read. After the shared reading exercise (*Colonial Life*, January, 2000), they wrote the correct tenses in their small booklets:

In 1607, a ship _____ with people from England _____ on the coast of the land we now

fill   land

call Virginia. With the permission of King James I of England, they _____ to start a

have set out

new life in a new land. With axes and spades they _____ a spot in the forest. They
clear

_____ a tiny village of mud huts. This village _____ Jamestown—the first successful

build   become

English settlement, or colony, in North America. Named after King James I, this new

village _____ a colony belonging to England: the people who _____ there were called
is   live

colonists.

Notice that there are different levels of complexity associated with the verbs. For instance, **regular past tense verbs** examples include *fill-filled* and *clear-cleared*. **Irregular past tense** refers to an irregular verb that is used very frequently: *is-was, build-built,* and *land-landed.*

In these examples, we have used shared reading as a structure to help the students gain a deeper understanding of social studies texts, figure out how the target language works, and analyze the structure on how the information is organized in a nonfiction text.

Theory-to-Practice Connection

Through the shared reading activities, students were able to analyze how language works in this genre. See Chapter 2.

SHARED WRITING

The purpose of shared writing is to help students to work as a group in the creation of a text. Rachel likes to do a shared writing activity after she takes her fourth-grade students on class trips, to help them learn to organize their ideas and write about their experiences. In this case, her purpose was to show her EL students how to gather and organize information to write an expository text and to integrate the new vocabulary they learned during the trip.

She decided beforehand what the objective of the shared writing activity was going to be: to organize their thoughts and report on what they learned during a visit to the New York Historical Society. The students saw an exhibit called "Nation at the Crossroads: The Great New York Debate Over the Constitution, 1787–88."

The teacher started by drawing a blank semantic web. As students checked their notes, they made suggestions about what they wanted to say. Rachael wanted to show the children that a great way to brainstorm for ideas is by creating a web where you list the things you want to write about (see Figure 5.17).

Figure 5.17 Semantic Map for Shared Writing

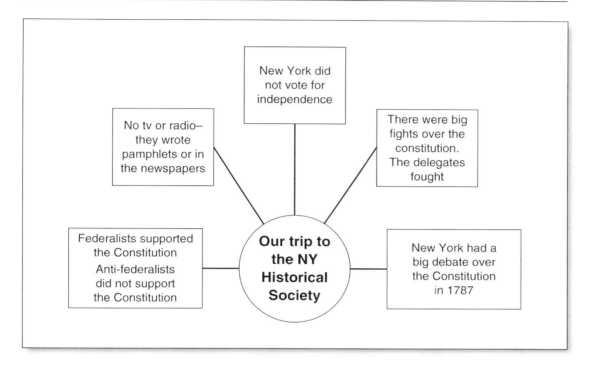

The teacher then helped the students to organize the piece they wanted to write. She asked guiding questions to help the children think about the organization of the text and decide what should go first and was important. For example, a student started talking about the bus ride to the Historical Society. Rachel redirected the discussion and asked the group to think about the purpose of the trip and focus only on the new things they learned at the Historical Society.

The group had a hard time deciding how to start the piece and what should go first. Then there were many arguments about how the ideas should go together. The teacher guided the discussions so that the piece would be cohesive. In this process, she is modeling how writing works and how to put ideas on paper using long sentences. She was also trying to show students how punctuation works. This is the collective piece the class wrote:

We learned many new things during our visit to the New York Historical Society. First we learned that during Colonial and Revolutionary times the only way to share information was through pamphlets and newspapers; they did not have other means of communicating. We also learned that New Yorkers were not supportive of the constitution at the beginning. They had big fights about it, and voted against it during the second Congress. The people in favor of the Constitution were Federalists. The people against the constitution were Anti-Federalists. They were afraid of too much government. It was not easy to get people to agree.

The teacher then asked the class to read the piece together, underlining the new words they had learned. She will use this same piece for a shared reading activity later on.

Theory-to-Practice Connection

Shared writing provides an opportunity for the teacher to model the process of writing, and shows students how academic language works, through a collaborative process in which students and teacher make decisions about how to put the ideas together. See Chapter 3.

CONCLUSION

In this chapter, we have provided a toolbox for teachers with ideas they can use to develop and expand the background knowledge and language skills of their ELs and struggling students at the same time that they expand their conceptual knowledge.

We start by giving examples of specific activities to develop background knowledge through the use of *audiovisuals*. We use *read aloud* to provide the students with information about the period and to introduce the major concepts of the unit without simplifying the content. *Shared reading* not only reinforces information, but it also helps students understand the structures of nonfiction texts and develop new language structures in context. Finally, through the use of *shared writing*, students understand how to organize their ideas to write expository texts. Throughout all these structures, we explore activities to increase *vocabulary and conceptual knowledge*.

TEACHER SELF-ASSESSMENT FOR THE UNIT

Have I . . .	
Created a planning chart for this unit integrating language and concept goals?	
Identified the key concepts that the students are expected to learn and thought about the structures I will use to teach those concepts?	
Used audiovisuals to facilitate the development of background knowledge?	
Used read aloud to anchor the unit of study and to increase the students' understanding of the concepts in this unit?	
Used scaffolding strategies to model and expand academic language, e.g., using different strategies to develop vocabulary in context?	
Planned classroom conversations around the read aloud at least twice weekly?	
Used graphic organizers to trigger background knowledge or to help students understand difficult concepts without heavy language load?	
Provided frequent and explicit feedback to the students?	
Used shared reading to work on syntax and text structures?	

Created enough opportunities for children to work collaboratively and have time to discuss and share ideas?	
Given enough language support to early stage EL students? Are they in three-way partnerships? Conferences? Peer work?	
Created thinking prompts that reflect the requirements of the unit; e.g., "The thought I have about this is. . ."?	
Developed a student assessment chart?	

6

Science Unit

Plant and Animal Adaptations
(Grades 5–6)

THE ENGLISH LANGUAGE LEARNER AND SCIENCE

All children are naturally interested in the world that surrounds them, and this curiosity is a powerful incentive in learning science. Their enthusiasm for this subject may bridge the barriers of language as they make new discoveries. In elementary school, science is often taught with hands-on experiments that can transform otherwise abstract phenomena into concrete, crystal-clear concepts (Dobb, 2004; Haynes & Zacarian, 2010). Language and science form a powerful link as children learn the new language in the process of their investigations. As students move up in the grades, their interest in this subject area begins to wane. The curriculum demands a deeper knowledge of abstract language and background knowledge; science becomes a challenging subject that many students do not have the skills to tackle (Chamot, 2009; Dong, 2004).

Manuel Hernandez, who teaches science to sixth-grade bilingual students, says,

> There is a big difference between teaching science in elementary school and in middle school. One of the biggest challenges is developing background knowledge for students who have little or no previous experience with the concepts needed to learn sixth-grade science. Many of my students do not have the reading skills needed to read the science textbooks or trade books that can support the concepts. I have to resort to alternative ways to present the content information and not rely solely on independent reading of the material or assuming that all my students can write a report on what they have seen or learned.

Even though Manuel is a science teacher, he realizes that he has to focus as much on the language structures and vocabulary that are part of this unit as on the scientific concepts that he wants to develop.

In this chapter, we aim to

- provide you with various activities that will help students develop background knowledge in order to understand the scientific concepts required by the unit;
- guide you in the process of teaching complex concepts using strategies that do not require an overload of language, without diluting the curriculum; and
- provide you with strategies to develop the technical language required by the unit.

For this unit, we are going to follow Manuel as he teaches a particularly challenging group of sixth graders. Manuel has 29 students in this class: 18 males and 11 females. Although his class is called "bilingual," not all of his students fit into the EL category, as many were born in the United States but have academic difficulties that prevented them from participating in the regular monolingual program. Since they have Hispanic names, they were placed in the bilingual program. Most of the students in this class function below grade level. There are four EL students who are recent immigrants from Mexico who read on a third-grade level. There are four shelters around the school, and some of the students have been moving from shelter to shelter since the school year started. Manuel is very committed to all of his students, but this particular group requires a lot of attention. He feels that this is the one chance they have to become engaged in their learning, and he wants them to love science. He thinks that if he inspires them, they will engage in other subjects as well. Other teachers who work with this group are very frustrated with their progress.

Here are some of the major challenges that Manuel faces as he plans the unit:

- Building **background knowledge**: The science curriculum is spiraling, meaning that it is cumulative. Information presented in one grade is taught again with more complexity in the next grade.
- Making the **content and the concepts** accessible to his students without an overload of language. Many of the children in the class have limited exposure to science, so Manuel needs to scaffold the unit.
- Developing the **technical and academic vocabulary** that the unit requires.
- Teaching children **how to use scientific procedures**, such as observing, classifying, describing, gathering data, making a hypothesis, and reporting.

This chapter presents many activities to scaffold your students so that they can understand the concepts of the unit. Given the constraints of time, you may not be able to follow all our suggestions. We are providing a toolbox of activities that you can adapt to your students' needs and to your particular time constraints.

PLANNING THE UNIT

This sample unit combines elements from both the fifth- and sixth-grade science curriculum in New York state, because many of Manuel's students did not study science in the fifth grade. The fifth-grade curriculum examines how plants and animals are connected in an ecosystem. The sixth-grade curriculum examines how animals and plants adapt to their environment. For our work in Manuel's class, we focused on the adaptations that have helped plants and animals to survive, and spotlighted ***thermoregulation***. Throughout this unit, we use visuals, shared reading, read aloud, and graphic organizers to develop background knowledge and concepts. In addition, we plan several research projects that students have to complete working in collaborative groups with their classmates. Through these group projects, students strengthen their understanding of the new concepts they are learning and develop the technical language they need to understand the content of this unit. We also organize a visit to the zoo and an experiment that can complement the understanding of the concept of adaptations.

Concepts and Teaching Tools

A very important process in our planning was to flush out the main concepts that Manuel wanted to teach and to figure out what teaching strategies he should use (see Table 6.1). The plans for this unit were made taking into consideration the need to use high-interest materials that do not have heavy language overload. Because many of his students did not have cumulative science knowledge from previous years, we knew we had to scaffold the unit using graphic organizers, a lot of visual aids, and ample opportunities to discuss and talk about what the students are learning.

The essential questions that students need to be able to answer at the end of the unit are:

- What are the mechanisms of adaptation that allow animals and plants to survive?
- What are the differences between behavioral and structural adaptations in animals?
- How do we gather and interpret information about animal and plant adaptations?
- How do scientists develop a hypothesis and analyze their data in order to confirm their thinking?

This unit will be taught in a 4-week period. The teacher sees his students twice a week for 45 minutes.

Table 6.1   Planning Concepts and Teaching Tools

Concepts	How Do I Teach Them?	How Do I Make Sure Students Understand?
Developing background knowledge: Animals and plants develop different kinds of mechanisms to survive	• Lesson • Visuals	• Venn diagram • Class discussion
Animal Adaptations • Structural ○ Thermoregulation • Behavioral	• Shared reading to support concepts • Class discussions • Vocabulary work: relating Tier 2 words to Tier 3 words • Interactive word wall to develop science vocabulary • Visit to Bronx Zoo and research projects • Read aloud	• Group research projects on adaptations • Note-taking • Summary organizer to synthesize ideas • Group research projects on adaptations before and after zoo visit

Concepts	How Do I Teach Them?	How Do I Make Sure Students Understand?
Plant Adaptations • Plants adapt to different habitats • We establish a hypothesis and do an experiment to prove if we are right o Desert plants absorb less water than tropical plants Scientists analyze data using statistical procedures: mean, median, mode, range	• Experiment • Math extension • Scaffold individual reports on adaptations	• Developing a hypothesis and analyzing results
Bringing concepts together		• Individual book reports for the unit

Table 6.2 includes content and language objectives.

Table 6.2 Content and Language Objectives

Content Goals	Curriculum of Talk: Thinking Skills	Target Vocabulary
Kinds of Questions That Will Guide Our Thinking		
5/3		*Comprehension*
Students will be able to understand the mechanisms of adaptation.	• Can you describe in your own words...?	• Mechanism • Environment • Survival • Habitats
5/17		*Analysis*
Students will be able to analyze through an experiment how plants adapt to their habitats.	• Can you describe the similarities or differences of...? • What is the evidence you have for...?	• Adaptation • Mutation • Thermoregulation • Hypothesis • Observation • Experiment
5/23		*Synthesis*
Students will integrate their new concepts by writing a science report on adaptations.	• Can you summarize...? • Can you explain...? • What ideas can you add to...?	• Conclusion • Mean • Mode • Range • Median

(Continued)

Table 6.2   (Continued)

Content Goals	Curriculum of Talk: Thinking Skills	Target Vocabulary
		Evaluation
	• What do you think about…? • Can you illustrate what you mean by…? • What is the most important…?	
Types of Conversations		

	• Whole-class discussions
	 • Student collaborative work
	 • Student presentations
	 • Partner work
		Conjunctions
		 • Cause and effect
		   o Because
		   o As a result
		   o Therefore
		 • Compare and contrast
		   o But
		   o However
		   o Yet
		   o Whereas

Theory-to-Practice Connection

Through these two charts the teacher identified his content objectives and established his language goals for this unit. See the introduction to Chapter 4.

BREAKING THE PLAN INTO DOABLE PARTS

Assessing and Developing Background Knowledge

For Manuel, it is very important that his students know the objective of what they are about to learn. Even though this is a practice that all children benefit from, for EL and struggling students it is particularly important because they need to clearly understand the whole purpose of the unit and not get lost in the individual parts. He introduces the unit, telling his students, "Today we are going to start with a unit that deals with animal and plant adaptations. All animals and plants live in habitats—this means environments— where they find shelter, food, and water that help them survive. But that is not enough for their continued survival; animals and plants also depend on their physical features and behavior in order to live. That is what we call adaptations." The teacher writes the words *habitats* and *adaptations* on the board. "First, we are going to study how animals and plants develop different kinds of mechanisms—that means ways in which their body adapts—to survive." He adds the word *survive* on the board. "We will spend some time reading and doing research about adaptations, and then we will learn about a very specific kind of adaptation in animals: thermoregulation." He adds the word *thermoregulation* and continues: "This will be a lot of fun because you are going to learn a lot of interesting facts in the process." He then tells his students that the words he has written on the board are going to be part of their individual dictionaries, and they will be added to their science word wall.

Visuals

Manuel starts teaching this unit with the aid of visuals so that the students can start making associations that will trigger background knowledge. In addition, he wants his students to expand their use of conjunctions when comparing and contrasting animals and plants that live in different environments (see Figure 6.3 on page 118). He posts these conjunctions on the board: *but*, *however*, *yet*, and *whereas*, and tells his students, "I want you to use these conjunctions when you are making comparisons, so that you can replace the boring '*and.*' For example, I am 5 feet 8 tall **whereas** Maria is 5 feet tall. I replaced the boring **and** with **whereas**."

Teacher	Animal and plants have different adaptations that help them survive. I will give you an example of what I mean; let's see if you can come up with others. Some animals are able to escape predators thanks to their wings, legs, or fins. For example, rabbits can escape predators because their hind legs are so strong.
Victor	The monkey has arms and a tail that allows him to swing from trees and escape!
Teacher	Good point. Can anyone think of an example about a plant?
Maria	How about the thorns in a rose, if you try to take them they pinch you.
Teacher	For the next few classes, we are going to talk about how plants and animals adapt to their environment in order to survive. Today, I am going to show you two pictures that show animals and two pictures that show plants. I want you to observe them carefully and tell me what is special about them. Remember that we are thinking about adaptation to the environment.
Teacher	Let's see if any of you can guess what is special about each of these sets of pictures. Look at the animals and then at the plants. Take a few minutes to observe the differences.

The teacher draws a Venn diagram on chart paper (Figure 6.4) to help students see the differences and similarities between the foxes, and then writes down what they say.

Teacher	Now that we see the differences in the foxes, can we figure out why these two foxes look so different?
Maria	The white one lives in the snow whereas the red one lives in the forest. You can't see the white one because it is the same color as the snow.

Figure 6.3   Illustrations to Analyze Adaptations

Source: Wikipedia free images.

Teacher   Great! You used one of the conjunctions I posted on the board. These are both foxes, but they look different. They have adapted to their habitat. The fur of the Arctic fox matches the habitat. The Arctic Fox lives in the North Pole (pointing to the map), the Arctic. If he blends into the snow, it protects itself from predators. Where do you think the other one lives?

Victor   The other fox lives in the forest. Is that why it is red and white?

Teacher   That is what I want you to find out. Please draw a Venn diagram in your notebooks and compare and contrast the two plants in the picture: One is a cactus and the other one is called elephant ears.

Figure 6.4 Venn Diagram Comparing and Contrasting Two Kinds of Foxes

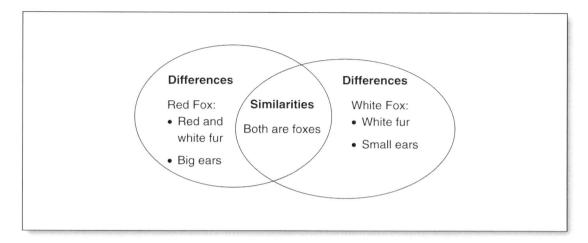

Differences

Red Fox:
- Red and
  white fur

- Big ears

Similarities

Both are foxes

Differences

White Fox:
- White fur

- Small ears

Theory-to-Practice Connection

Here the teacher is developing background knowledge at the same time that he is working on a specific language goal: the use of compare-and-contrast conjunctions. See Chapter 1.

Figure 6.5 shows an example of Maria's diagram.

Figure 6.5 Maria's Venn Diagram

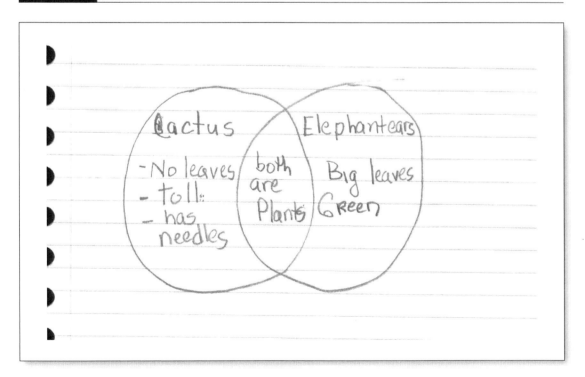

Maria	One is a cactus. It lives in the desert. The other one has a big green leaf. I think one can be without water and the other needs lots of water.
Teacher	Great observations. The cactus is a plant that adapts to very arid—dry—environments. It can survive with very little water. On the other hand, this leafy plant, called elephant ears, is very green and lush. Where do you think it would live?
Maria	In a sunny place with water.
Teacher	Yes, this plant needs a lot of sun and good water. It would grow in the tropics. This is an example of how plants have adapted to very different conditions in their habitats. In the green plant, the leaves are big and they are facing down so that the water slides off and does not rot the leaves. In the tropics it rains a lot. One has adapted to dry conditions, and one to having lots of water.

The teacher asks his students to think about ways in which they have seen animals and plants adapt to the conditions of their environment. He is surprised by how much more the students know about adaptations than he had thought:

Manuel	How about the polar bear and the black bear? Do they adapt to their surroundings just like the fox?
Juan	The whales adapt to the cold weather because they have blubber in their bodies. That is how they can survive. So do the penguins.
Iris	In the Dominican Republic, we have huge ferns in the woods. They are almost the size of trees, here they are small—my mother has a hanging plant—fern—it is almost a different plant from the ones we have. That is adaptation, right?
Miriam	How about living in the water? I saw it in a picture of a water lily. Only special plants can grow in the water.

Manuel then asks the students to do some research to find out what are the adaptations that the red fox has made to its environment and to figure out why the ears are different sizes and shapes in both foxes. He has taken several books on adaptations out of the library and in addition he tells the students they can look up information on the Internet in the school library. The websites that he is using are Brainpop (www.brainpop.com), Teacher Domain (www.teacherdomain.com), and National Geographic (www.nationalgeographic.com). To do this work, he pairs students in three-way partnerships so that students who have more reading difficulties can work with students better able to do the research.

Throughout this lesson, Manuel has provided his students with some information about the concept of adaptations using visual aides that have triggered their background knowledge. At the same time, he has engaged them in organizing their own observations using a Venn diagram. Finally, he has extended the lesson by asking his students to do research on the environmental adaptations that the foxes have made.

SHARED READING

The teacher knows that his students need to get some information from their textbook, but the information is at a level higher than what they can read. He wants the students to learn

Figure 6.6 Shared Reading for Plant and Animal Adaptations

Different Kinds of Adaptations in Animals and Plants

Animal Adaptations

Structural adaptations

Animals and plants have made adaptations that help them survive in their habitats. Some adaptations are **structural**. This means that the adaptations are physical features. Some examples of structural adaptations in animals are **thermoregulation**, which allow animals such as camels to regulate their body temperature to deal with extreme hot weather conditions. Another structural adaptation is the fur of animals. There are many other kinds of structural adaptations. Can you think of any others?

Behavioral adaptations

Behavioral adaptations are what animals do in order to survive. For example, during the winter months many animals sleep and use their body fat to survive instead of food. This is called **hibernation**. Another kind of behavioral adaptation is **migration**. Birds migrate to warmer climates during the winter. Some animals exhibit both structural and behavioral adaptations.

Plant Adaptations

Plants also have to adapt to extreme weather conditions. Some plants, like the cactus, have adapted to the desert, where there is hardly any water. The stems of the cactus expand when there is rain and it uses the water little by little. The roots of many cacti extend over a large area to be able to collect water. Another way that cactus have of conserving water is by having narrow and small leaves. The smaller the leaf is, the less evaporation. Other plants grow in the sun under normal weather and watering conditions, and they adapt to this kind of environment by growing big roots and leafy leaves. Other plants grow in the water. They have very poor or no roots. Water lilies belong to this group.

Why do adaptations occur?

Adaptations occur because of the **mutations (changes) of genes**. This happens by accident. Some mutations are good as they make the animal better able to survive. For example, rabbits tend to have many offspring, but those that have stronger hind legs, which help them run the fastest, have a better chance to escape predators, live longer, and have offspring with strong hind legs.

When animals and plants cannot adapt to the environment they become **extinct.**

---

the concepts and decides to summarize the information and present it as a shared reading activity. At the end of this, the students will have a copy of the same text and will go back to their desks to read and underline the parts that they think are more important, as they will use this information later on when they work in groups (see Figure 6.6). As he reads and invites the students to read with him, he will give explanations on the run of the challenging vocabulary and point out the main ideas.

Figure 6.7 Shared Reading Word Webs

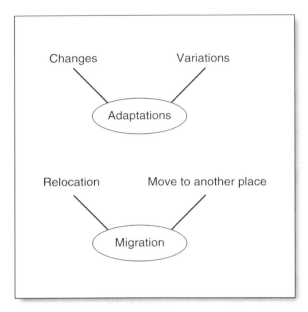

Manuel reads the entire text first and then invites the students to read specific paragraphs, stopping to point out the main idea each time. He also stops before each heading to point out the features of a nonfiction text: What are the roles of headings and subheadings? Can students predict what they are going to read from reading the subheadings? Then he works on the vocabulary, writing all the Tier 3 vocabulary (bold in Figure 6.6) on the board and giving explanations on the run. These Tier 3 words will be added to the science word wall. Later on, he goes over the vocabulary, connecting the new words with Tier 2 words to help students remember them. Figure 6.7 shows two examples.

After the shared reading activity, the students are divided into four groups. There are many books about animals on each table. Two groups do research on animal adaptations, and two groups do research on plant adaptations. The research will take time, and it will be part of a group report. To help them organize their thinking, the teacher gives them graphic organizers to structure their information (see Table 6.8).

After the students finish their research, each group reports on its findings. Students have copied the information they found in the books.

Through these activities, the teacher was able to focus his students' attention on the different features that animals have and how these can be to an animal's advantage in its habitat.

Table 6.8 Student Research Projects

Animals (Marsupials)	Structural Adaptations	Behavioral Adaptations	Because of These Adaptations, the Animals Can . . .
Opossums	• Long claws	• They smell like a sick or dead animal when in danger	• Deter predators
Gliding Opossums	• Long tail to hang around tree branches • Their skin stretches from wrist to ankle and acts as a slide	• Stay high in trees • Babies are born premature. They stay in pouch and suck milk in the mother's pouch and are there for long time	• Go up trees to avoid predators • Fly from tree to tree • Are on their own when they are able to survive • Stay with their moms until they are old enough to function
Kangaroos	• Back legs very strong—can run up to 35 miles per hour	• Run fast on two legs	• Escape predators

Animals (Birds)	Structural Adaptations	Behavioral Adaptations	Because of These Adaptations, the Animals Can . . .
Penguins	• Camouflage: Color-black and white. From the bottom of the sea they are not seen because they are white, from the top they blend with the water • Thick feathers • Blubber under skin	• Move in groups to stay warm	• Avoid predators in the water • Survive the cold
Ducks	• Webbed feet	• Migration	• Use their feet like paddles • Go to warmer places in winter and survive

Habitats (Plants)	Structural Adaptations	Because of This, the Plants Can . . .
• Desert: Hot and dry • Cactus	• The stems expand • Instead of leaves they have thorns	• Store water • Do not lose water through leaves
• Tropical rainforest: Wet and sometimes dark in the ground	• Big leaves • Some grow high on trees	• Allow them to get rid of too much water • Capture the sun

The students gathered some information through shared reading, and then they worked in groups to do additional, more in-depth research. Next, they classified the information and analyzed the data to draw their conclusions. Finally, they had to describe the results to the rest of the class.

Theory-to-Practice Connection

The teacher adapted a difficult text to meet the linguistic needs of his students but made sure that he did not water down the content of the unit. See Chapter 1.

Making Inferences and Drawing Conclusions

Manuel has arranged for his class to visit the Bronx Zoo. To plan for this trip, he has adapted information that he downloaded from the Birmingham Zoo website (http://www.birminghamzoo.com/).

The purpose of the visit is for his students to observe an animal and discover the adaptations that help that animal to survive. In preparation for the trip, he asks his students to choose an animal from a list he has gotten on the Bronx Zoo website (http://www.bronxzoo.com/

animals-and-exhibits/animals.aspx) and to research its habitat. The students work in groups to choose the animals and then help each other read information about the habitat of the animal. There are six groups, and they choose the following animals:

Group 1   Anaconda

Group 2   Lion

Group 3   Gorilla

Group 4   Lemur

Group 5   Hippopotamus

Group 6   Giraffe

The students have an organizer to write down the information about their animal. First, they write down what they have found; and then, during their visit to the zoo, they fill in the information they are gathering from their observations. After the visit, Manuel asks his students to analyze the characteristics of the animals and to think which of these may not help in the survival of the animal. Table 6.9 gives one example.

Table 6.9 Template for Zoo Visit

Before the Visit to the Zoo	During the Visit	After the Visit
→	→	→
Animal: ANACONDA		
Habitat	*Adaptations*	*Problems*
Write down information about the habitat of the animal.	What are the characteristics that *you notice* that have helped the animal to adjust to its environment?	Write down the characteristics that you think may not help the animal survive.
• They live near rivers and swamps in the Amazon jungle and other places in South America • Tropical rainforest • They like to be under water to catch their prey • They prefer swampy water to hide under leaves and branches	• The skin can look like part of the surroundings, so it looks like a tree trunk. • The skin allows them to camouflage. It is brown with a little green and it has black spots • They cover with vegetation in swamps to mimic vegetation • It mainly hunts at night • The eyes and mouth are on top of the head so they can breath waiting underwater • It has a huge mouth to eat big animals, big jaw that opens up as big as it has to, it is elastic	• It is too big and it cannot move fast to escape when attacked on land • The head is small, if an animal grabs the head it will kill the snake • If it eats a big animal in the water it cannot move, an alligator can eat it

What Do You Think?

From the information you gathered about this animal and your observations, what are your conclusions about its chances for survival?

The anaconda has great chances for survival because it is stronger than most animals and it has very few predators.

Through this activity, Manuel has asked his students to examine one specific animal in depth, **researching** its habitat and **observing** its physical characteristics during a trip to the zoo. Finally, he has asked them to **make inferences** and to **draw conclusions** from their observations. Since most of the work has been done in groups, students have had opportunities to talk about their projects and exchange ideas.

Theory-to-Practice Connection

Through this activity students, working in groups, were able to exchange ideas and practice discussing an academic topic, which required the use of critical thinking skills. See Chapter 2.

DEVELOPING CRITICAL THINKING SKILLS THROUGH READ ALOUD

The read aloud focuses on three aspects: an anticipatory guide to trigger background knowledge, vocabulary work, and note taking to reinforce concepts.

The teacher decides that he wants his students to focus in depth on one kind of adaptation: *thermoregulation*. To anchor the concept of thermoregulation, he decides to focus on camels since they use this mechanism. He will read a book entitled *Camels* (Wexo, 1999).

Anticipatory Guide

Before he starts the book, he gives his students an **anticipatory guide** (Reiss, 2008). This guide helps the students to draw upon prior knowledge and to recognize how their own point of view can change after they are confronted with facts. Manuel wants his students to compare their ideas before the read aloud with the new concepts they have gained through listening to the book. Students write their ideas before the read aloud and finish completing the guide after the read aloud (see Table 6.10). A full-sized blank version of the Anticipatory Guide is available at http://www.corwin.com/connectingcontent4ell. Each student has to fill out his or her own guide.

Table 6.10 Anticipatory Guide for *Camels* (Wexo, 1999)

Camels . . .	My Belief Before the Read Aloud and Discussion	What I Learned
Live in the U.S.		
Carry an extra supply of water in their humps		
Never sweat		
Need to drink water every day		
Can go a long time without drinking or eating		
Can adapt to very high temperatures		

Doing the anticipatory guide gives the teacher a sense of his students' knowledge about the subject at the same time that it gives the students a strong motivation to listen attentively to see if they were right.

Vocabulary Work

Manuel selects a key word for the understanding of the book and the concept: *thermoregulation*. He discusses the two parts that make the word: *thermo-* and *-regulation*.

Teacher	The word *thermo* means heat. Can you think of other words that start with *thermo*?
Damaris	Like thermometer.
Pedro	(Hesitantly) Like thermos for the coffee?
Teacher	That is right. A thermometer measures heat, like when you have a fever, and a thermos keeps hot what you put inside. Now, can you get an idea about what *regulation* means? What is another word that is like *regulation*?

He puts the word in the center of a web and adds words as the students speak. He lets them look in their thesaurus, and as the students find equivalent words such as *rules*, *control*, and *adjustment*, he adds them to the web. He then adds the words to the science word wall.

Teacher	The word *thermoregulation* means heat control.

He follows the same process with five other words that he thinks are essential for understanding the book.

Theory-to-Practice Connection

The teacher has carefully selected the key vocabulary that will help students understand the book, and he has chosen to teach the words in clusters to make sure his students make lasting connections. See Chapter 1.

Note Taking

Manuel wants his students to take notes as he reads; he knows that this is an essential skill the students will need increasingly as they move up in the grades. ELs need formats and techniques that scaffold this process. He is using a template other teachers in his school have used before, the Cornell Note-Taking System (Pauk & Owens, 2007), shown in Figure 6.11. A full-sized blank version of the Template for Note Taking is available at http://www.corwin.com/connectingcontent4ell. This template has two columns. The left column is used for listing the main idea of the first four paragraphs. The fifth space on the column is left blank so that the students can practice adding the main idea of the fifth paragraph. After each paragraph, the teacher gives students time to fill in details. Using this template will allow his students to study their notes and to test their knowledge by covering the right-hand side.

Figure 6.11 Template for Note Taking

Topic	Details
What happens to humans when it's hot?	1. humans sweat to cool of 2. need water 3.
What happens to camels when it's too hot?	1. their temperature gos up 2. they dont sweat 3. they don't need water
What does a camel's hump have inside?	1. fat (for energy) 2. not water. 3.
What happens to a camel when it hasn't had water for some time?	1. they use the fat in hump 2. they become thin 3. they have a hollow hole in the ribs
Definition of Thermo-regulation	1. It is when the temp. goes u- 2. It adjusts to the weather 3. themo — heat
Summary	I think thermoregulation is.... when the body temperature goes up because is hot outside, like the camel their body temp. can go up 6°F

Source: Cornell Note-Taking System (Pauk & Owens, 2007).

As Manuel reads, he gives a listening prompt before each paragraph.

Teacher Listen carefully. What happens to humans if our bodies get too hot?

Humans can die if their bodies get too hot. This is why people sweat when the air around them gets warmer than their bodies. As the sweat evaporates, it cools the body and helps to keep it cooler than the surrounding air.

Source: Camels by John Bonnet Wexo (1999).

He allows his students time to take notes and then draws their attention to the next important concept. *"What happens to camels when it gets too hot? This is where thermoregulation is described."*

Camels don't sweat as easily as people do. When the air temperature rises, a camel just lets its own body temperature rise as well. This way the camel doesn't start to sweat until the air gets really hot—and this saves a lot of water. A camel can let its body temperature rise six degrees Fahrenheit without hurting itself.

Source: Camels by John Bonnet Wexo (1999).

Students turn to their partners to consult with each other as they write their notes. Manuel asks them questions that make them think deeply about the information they are receiving.

Teacher   Take a few minutes to discuss what happens to humans and camels when the temperature gets hot.

The questions that he asks (see Table 6.12) require that the students think through their answers.

Table 6.12   Thinking Skills During Read Aloud

Summarizing	What did we learn today about thermoregulation in camels?
Synthesis	Can we think of how thermoregulation works in other animals? How about dogs?
Analyzing	How is thermoregulation a mechanism of adaptation?
Evaluating	Why do you think that it is important to know about thermoregulation?

After the read aloud, students review their anticipation guide. Not surprisingly, most students have misconceptions about where camels keep water stored. They have discovered that their humps are not to store water but fat.

Through this read aloud, students were able to understand the process of thermoregulation. In addition, they used the following critical thinking skills: summarizing, synthesizing, analyzing, and evaluating.

Theory-to-Practice Connection

When teachers model thinking skills during read aloud, they are providing students with clear examples of the kind of thinking they should be engaged in during independent reading. See Chapter 3.

EXPERIMENT: PLANT ADAPTATIONS

HOW THE SHAPES OF LEAVES CHANGE ACCORDING TO THE HABITAT (DESERT AND TROPICAL PLANTS)

Manuel incorporates an experiment that shows how the habitat influences the shape of plant leaves. This will help his students to form a clearer understanding of plant adaptations. In addition, he wants to guide the students through the process of scientific inquiry. He wants his students to

1. observe;

2. establish a hypothesis;

3. test the hypothesis with an experiment;

4. classify and categorize the information (through graphs); and

5. report the findings.

1. Observe

The teacher explains that an experiment helps us test an idea in a careful, orderly manner. The first step is observing closely and asking, *Why?* This is a scientific question, and it has to be answered by gathering evidence. He gives each table a collection of leaves he has gathered and a set of pictures depicting different desert and rainforest plants. Then, he adds *that "sometimes leaves don't look like what we think of as a typical leaf; for example, cacti have spines and these are their modified leaves."* The students spend a few minutes observing the samples and the pictures of plants and their habitat. He encourages his students to talk with each other and write all the differences that they noticed in a chart that he has provided (Table 6.13). He is asking students to categorize plants according to the shape of their leaves.

Table 6.13 Leaf Classification

Plants	Leaf Sizes	Habitats
Palmers' Agave	Long with spines	Desert, Mexico, Arizona
Aloe	Long elongated	Desert, Southwest
Saguaro	Spines	Arizona desert
Barrel Cactus	Spines	Desert, Southwest
Hibiscus	Round, big	Tropics, Florida
Coleus	Round, big	Tropics, Florida
Elephant Ears	Round, big	Tropics, Florida

The class then follows the following process:

1. The students make several observations:
    o Tropical plants have bigger leaves.
    o Most desert plants have long elongated leaves or spines.

2.   They need to figure out the reason for those differences:
     o   Students need to come up with a "theory" of why leaves are so different in these two environments.
     o   They have to make a hypothesis taking into account the information they have gathered.

2. Establish a Hypothesis

Manuel explains that a hypothesis is like a prediction. *"The difference is that a hypothesis can be tested."* He writes on the board the language structure that he wants students to use:

If _____ then _____ because _____

Then he models a hypothesis for the students:

If we stop watering a plant, then the plant will die because it needs water to live.

The students get an opportunity to practice making a hypothesis:

If we put a plant in a dark closet, **then** the plant will die **because** it needs light to live.

The teacher asks the students to make a hypothesis about their observations. He tells them to go back to their charts and discuss in their tables the differences in size and habitats in rainforest plants and desert plants.

After a while, the students are ready to make a hypothesis. The teacher writes on chart paper what the students dictate:

If desert plants have smaller leaves **then** they will conserve more water **because** there is little rain in the desert.

If tropical plants have bigger leaves **then** they will absorb more water **because** it rains a lot.

Figure 6.14   Cardboard Leaves for Experiment

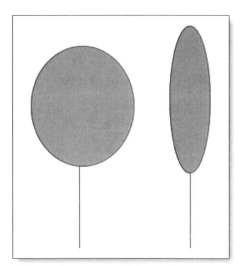

3. Test the Hypothesis With an Experiment

This experiment is designed to show, using cardboard leaves, that the shape of the leaf has a lot to do with the absorption of water (see Figure 6.14). Every student receives two pieces of cardboard of the same size. Using both pieces, they have to cut an oval and a round shape of the same size. The students place their cardboard leaves in measuring cups, each containing 500 ml of water with the cardboard touching the water. The cups sit on a tray. A wooden stem is glued to one of the extremes of each of the cardboard leaves. Each table makes one set of "leaves." The measuring cup is covered with plastic wrap to avoid evaporation and with a small hole where the "stem" is inserted. All the measuring cups are placed on a tray in the same place in the class.

4. Classify and Categorize the Information

After 2 days, the students come back to the class and record how much water each individual cardboard leaf has absorbed. They will have to subtract the amount of water left in the container from the initial 500 ml. The students record the results in a table (Table 6.15).

Table 6.15 Results for Water Absorption

Table	Ml of Water Lost in the Narrow Leaf (out of 500 ml)	Ml of Water Lost in the Broad Leaf (out of 500 ml)
Table 1	100	150
Table 2	102	120
Table 3	110	125
Table 4	100	135
Table 5	105	135

5. Report the Findings

Each table reports the findings, and the teacher asks the students to review their hypothesis. He rereads the hypothesis he wrote on chart paper:

If desert plants have smaller leaves **then** they will conserve more water **because** there is little rain in the desert.

If tropical plants have bigger leaves **then** they will absorb more water **because** it rains a lot.

Theory-to-Practice Connection

The teacher has used a specific language prompt associated with making a hypothesis to channel the students' thinking in a specific way. See Chapter 2.

The students have confirmed their hypothesis, but Manuel wants to push their thinking. He asks, *"What has happened to the water? Where has it gone? Has it disappeared?"*

Gloria   The cardboard leaves.

Teacher   The leaves absorbed the water. The round leaves absorbed more water, and the oval ones absorbed less.

The teacher reviews the steps that the class has taken to do this experiment:

1. They observed and organized their observations.

2. They established a hypothesis.

3. They performed an experiment to test their hypothesis.

4. They classified and organized the information on a graph.

5. They reported their findings.

6. Their hypothesis was proven correct.

Through this experiment, Manuel has shown his students how the scientific process works and has taken them through a cycle where they observed and classified the different shapes of leaves. Furthermore, they made a hypothesis about the reason for the differences. Finally, the students proved their hypothesis through an experiment.

Math Extension

Manuel decides to extend this lesson so that he can review some math concepts. He wants the students to practice calculating **mean**, **median**, **mode**, and **range**. Students work in groups to do the calculations. The teacher knows that this interaction is very helpful to the students whose computational skills are weak or who struggle with the concepts.

He explains to his students that figuring out the mean, the median, and the mode allows us to look at data in different ways: *"**Mean** tells us about the average of all numbers."* He gives an example of mean: *"We have 4 sixth-grade classes in the school. Two classes have 29 students, one class has 30 students, and one class has 18 students. If we want to figure the mean we add all the numbers."* He adds 29 + 29 + 30 + 18 = 106. *"Then, we divide this number 106 by the number of classes: 4. That number would be 26.5. We have an average of 26.5 students per sixth-grade class in the school. That is the **mean**."*

He asks his students to figure out the mean for each set of cardboard leaves. The students work in groups and compute the results.

101 for the narrow leaves, 115 for the broad leaves

The teacher places those results in a chart under **mean** (see Table 6.16).

The teacher then tells his students that now they are going to find the **median**. This is the middle value in a list of numbers. To figure this out, you list all the numbers from each set of leaves in order from small to large. He writes on the board as students dictate the following numbers:

Narrow leaves   100, 100, 102, 105, 110

Broad leaves   120, 125, 135, 135, 150

He asks students which is the middle number in each set. The students correctly identify 102 and 135. The teacher then tells them that they have found the **median**. He places the results in the chart.

He now wants the students to find the mode on their own. *"Now, I'm going to give you a definition, and you need to figure it out. The **mode** is the number that shows more often. Can you figure out what is the mode in the two sets of leaves?"*

Students provide the correct answer: 100 and 135.

Finally, the teacher focuses on the concept of **range**. *"Range tells us if all the results are grouped together or if they are very spread out. It is the difference between the* *smallest and the biggest number. In our experiment, it tells us how different the results were for each set of leaves.*" He asks his students to subtract the lowest from the highest number. The result for the narrow leaf is 10 and for the broad leaf is 30. He adds this data to the chart (see Table 6.16). Now, the students can see the data for their experiment reflected in different ways.

Table 6.16 Data for the Plant Experiment

	Narrow Leaves	**Broad Leaves**
Median	102	135
Mode	100	135
Range	10	30
Mean	101	115

Once the students have completed the table, the teacher allows them time to draw some conclusions from the information.

Teacher   Based on the range of the two sets of data, what can we see?

Isabel   The narrow leaf is more clustered.

Gustavo   The broad leaf is more spread out.

Teacher   Can you think why?

Margarita   Maybe because the broad leaves, like some are a bit bigger. When we cut the cardboard, some are bigger.

Guadalupe   Perhaps that is the reason. Some of the broader cardboard leaves were bigger and they absorbed more water, so the range is more bigger . . . spread out.

By applying the concepts of mode, median, range, and mean, Manuel is allowing his students to analyze the results and to figure out explanations for the results. This is part of the scientific process.

Source: Mini lesson adapted from Southwest Center for Education and the Natural Environment, http://scene.asu.edu

INDIVIDUAL BOOK REPORTS

At the end of this unit, students are asked to write a book report to show their understanding of plant and animal adaptations. They are given a clear format they must follow (see Table 6.17).

Table 6.17 Book Report Format

Book Report

You should cover why adaptations happen and provide examples. Your book report will consist of *a minimum of 10 pages*, excluding *the title page*. Each page will be different, so follow directions carefully. Put a checkmark in the space to the left of each item once you have completed *that part* of your report.

Areas you *must* cover:

- ☐ Table of contents.

- ☐ Introduction: Describe what your report is going to cover. You can use the information below to create your summary.

- ☐ Give your own definition of adaptations.

- ☐ Explain why adaptations happen.

- ☐ Give examples of adaptations in both animals and plants.

- ☐ Describe a *structural* or **behavioral** adaptation in an animal in detail.

- ☐ Describe thermoregulation in an animal other than a camel.

- ☐ Describe a plant adaptation. You can use the information you got from the experiment in class.

- ☐ Add an adaptation that we have not covered in class, it could be mimicry, or camouflage in insects, or you could zero in on an animal (such as penguins) that exhibits both behavioral and structural adaptations. Follow your interest.

- ☐ Conclusion.

- ☐ Bibliography: List the books or websites you have used for this report.

Copyright © 2011 by Corwin. All rights reserved. Reprinted from *Connecting Content and Academic Language for English Learners and Struggling Students, Grades 2–6*, by Ruth Swinney and Patricia Velasco. Thousand Oaks, CA: Corwin, www.corwin.com. Reproduction authorized only for the local school site or nonprofit organization that has purchased this book.

Manuel knows that not all the students can do the book reports independently. He gathers those students who need more support and scaffolds the process by giving them preprinted pages with parts of the report written, so that they can do the research and learn the concepts. Table 6.18 shows examples of a couple of the pages.

Table 6.18 Scaffolded Book Reports

My book report is about

_____

_____.

In this report I write about the following kinds of adaptations

_____

_____.

To complete this report I have done research on _____and

_____ adaptations, focusing on

_____.

I also learned about thermoregulation in

_____

_____.

Finally, I researched _____adaptations

in_____.

I was interested in this adaptation because

_____

_____.

(Continued)

Table 6.18 (Continued)

I believe that adaptations occur because

_____

_____.

Some adaptations can be good because

_____

_____.

Other adaptations can be harmful because

_____

_____.

One adaptation that I found particularly interesting is

_____

_____.

Animals that cannot adapt to the environment

_____

_____.

Here are some examples of animals that were not able to adapt to

_____

_____

_____

_____.

The most interesting fact I found is

_____

_____.

Three things that I want to remember are

_____

_____

_____.

Copyright © 2011 by Corwin. All rights reserved. Reprinted from *Connecting Content and Academic Language for English Learners and Struggling Students, Grades 2–6*, by Ruth Swinney and Patricia Velasco. Thousand Oaks, CA: Corwin, www.corwin.com. Reproduction authorized only for the local school site or nonprofit organization that has purchased this book.

CONCLUSION

In this chapter, we have scaffolded the concept of adaptations, suggesting several activities that will help EL and struggling students to develop the critical thinking skills that are necessary for understanding science concepts. Much of the learning has been done by the students working in collaborative groups. This not only helps students understand or refine the new concepts that they are learning, but it also develops the language skills they need for this unit.

We used shared reading and read aloud to present and reinforce concepts that students could not access on their own. In addition, we helped the students develop note-taking skills in order to help them integrate the information. At the end of each of those activities, students had to practice their new learning by doing work on their own or in groups. Students were involved in several research projects where they had to put together reports and present them to the class, integrating critical thinking skills such as summarizing and synthesizing information and finding cause and effect. We also included an experiment using the process of scientific inquiry and analyzing the results using basic statistical concepts. In this way, we integrated some math concepts into the unit.

Finally, students had to apply their research skills on a book report that covers the material taught in the unit. The report is scaffolded for students who need additional support.

TEACHER SELF-ASSESSMENT FOR THE UNIT

Have I . . .	
Created plans for organizing the concepts and language goals?	
Identified the key concepts that the students are expected to learn and thought about the structures I will use to teach those concepts?	
Used visuals to facilitate the development of background knowledge?	
Used shared reading to teach and reinforce concepts?	
Used read aloud to help students understand new concepts?	
Incorporated note-taking skills?	
Used graphic organizers to trigger background knowledge, or to help students understand difficult concepts without heavy language load?	
Created enough opportunities for children to work collaboratively and have time to discuss and share ideas?	
Incorporated the steps of scientific inquiry in the experiment, allowing students to interpret the information?	
Provided opportunities for independent research?	

7

Thematic Unit

The Rainforest (Grades 2–3)

THE ENGLISH LANGUAGE LEARNER AND THEMATIC UNITS

Thematic planning emphasizes the interdisciplinary nature of learning; it asserts the relationship between reading, writing, science, and math by connecting all the content areas through the exploration of a broad topic. These characteristics of thematic instruction are invaluable for EL and struggling students since they can build upon the concepts and language they are learning and use their background knowledge (Freeman & Freeman, 2000, 2009). Students can transfer the knowledge they are gaining from one curriculum area to the other and pursue their own interests as they delve deeper into the topic. This planning provides many opportunities for children to make connections across different subject areas and to learn new vocabulary and language structures that they can use across the day in meaningful ways (Lipson, Valencia, Wixson, & Peters, 1993).

This kind of planning has many advantages for EL and struggling students:

- It allows the students to focus on an area of study in depth.
- It emphasizes the development of thinking skills that students can use across the content areas.
- It provides students with extensive opportunities to use and practice the new language they are learning throughout the day and throughout the duration of the unit.
- Students at different levels of academic and linguistic development can delve into the topic at their own levels of understanding.
- It promotes collaborative learning.

In this chapter, we aim to

- provide you with a step-by-step plan to develop a thematic unit that will cover the major curricular areas: language arts, science, social studies, and math;
- guide you in the process of teaching complex concepts and critical thinking skills that students can apply across the different disciplines; and
- provide an array of activities that cover the range of major curricular areas, focusing on the development of vocabulary and language structures.

Jackie O'Neil teaches a self-contained ESL bridge class composed of second- and third-grade students in a suburban school in New Jersey. Jackie has 25 students who are second language learners at different stages of language acquisition and at different levels of academic performance. Sixteen of her students are Spanish-speaking from Mexico and the Dominican Republic; four students are from Brazil and speak Portuguese; three students are from Poland, speaking Polish; and two students are from Haiti and speak Haitian Creole. In terms of academic performance, there is a wide range of abilities in the class. Thirteen students read at or above grade level in their native languages and have had uninterrupted schooling in their native countries before coming to the United States. The rest of the students read below grade level; two students have had very little prior schooling. When we visited Jackie for the first time, she said, "*I have in this room 25 children that not only have a wide range of abilities and languages but are in two grade levels. There are some students that are very advanced and are ready to do work above their grade level; other students can barely do grade-level work. I am supposed to teach all of them grade-appropriate curriculum, even if they do not understand English well. I have no support from anyone else in the school; my administrators act as if we were invisible. There is no way that I could reach all my kids without planning a curriculum that will allow each child to find an area that they can connect to and feel passionate about. Thematic planning is the only way that I could meet the needs of such a diverse group. I need to help my students to master not only the content areas, but also English and literacy skills. To be successful, I have to integrate reading and writing with science and social studies and even with math. It is the best way for the children to make sense of what they are learning.*"

Here are some of the major challenges that Jackie faces as she plans this unit:

- Building background knowledge
- Helping students to do research and read informational texts in English without full proficiency in the language
- Developing the technical and academic vocabulary that the unit requires
- Teaching children how to find information and organize their ideas
- Teaching children how to write down and express what they are learning
- Developing the critical thinking skills needed for this topic

This chapter presents many activities to scaffold your students so that they can understand the concepts of the unit. Given the constraints of time, you may not be able to follow all our suggestions. We are providing a toolbox of activities that you can adapt to your students' needs and to your particular time constraints.

PLANNING THE UNIT

Jackie decided on a broad theme, "The Rainforest," because she felt that most of her students could connect to the theme, as they came from tropical places close to the Equator. Through this theme, she can cover part of the social studies and science scope and sequence for second and third grade: diversity of life and habitats in communities around the world. For language arts, she feels that this unit will teach her students how to read and write nonfiction texts, and this is a wonderful opportunity to build background knowledge. She thinks that there are enormous advantages to teaching nonfiction reading by involving children in a deep study of a theme.

Jackie knows that for a thematic unit to be successful, it has to be planned around questions that can be answered from multiple perspectives and using different kinds of information.

For this unit, her essential questions are:

- What is a rainforest?
- How do rainforests work?
- What is the importance of the rainforest in maintaining life on Earth?

Jackie has planned the unit's goals around these questions, providing her students with the information and resources they need. Her goals for the unit are as follows:

1. Students will understand that the rainforest is vital to sustain variety of life on Earth.

2. Students will gain an understanding of the interrelationship between living things and their environment in the rainforest.

3. Students will gain an understanding of the forces threatening the rainforest.

Table 7.1 Learning Goals for Each Curriculum Area

Social Studies	Science	Language Arts	Math	Art
• Geographical concepts ○ The Equator ○ Tropical forests around the world • Interdependence • Human impact on the rainforest • Study of people that live in the rainforest	• Characteristics of rainforest as an ecosystem ○ Climate ○ Layers ○ Variety of plant and animal life • Camouflage • Terrarium	• Reading non-fiction texts ○ Main idea ○ Inferencing ○ Predicting ○ Understanding author's purpose • Writing non-fiction ○ Journals ○ Book reports: ○ My book about the rainforest • Writing a play	• Subtraction • Using information to make graph charts • Concepts of > and <	• Drawing layers of the rainforest • Drawing in book reports

Table 7.2 Concept Planning Chart

Concepts	How Do I Teach Them?	How Do I Make Sure Students Understand?
	Tools	**Activities**
Developing background knowledge • What is a rainforest?	• Video: *Travel to the Rainforest* (www.thewildclassroom.com)	• Note-taking graphic organizers • Group work
What are the most important characteristics of the rainforest? • Layers • Climate • Location • Animal and plant variety	• Pictures, visuals, and picture books • Demonstrations • Read alouds • Research projects • Bar graphs	• Comparing rain in rainforest with rainfall in NJ • Research projects on layers and drawings • Observations and notes on terrariums • Collaborative projects and presentations • Building a terrarium to simulate a rainforest
Identify rainforests around the world	• Globe • World map	• Identifying the rainforests around the world
In-depth study of animals and plants of the rainforest • Camouflage	• Read aloud • Shared reading	• Book reports
Threats to the rainforest	• Read aloud: *The Great Kapok Tree* • Writing a play	• Producing the play
Learning about people of the rainforest	• Student research projects	• Book reports

Language Goals for the Unit

Curriculum of Talk	Language Prompts	Vocabulary
• Class discussions • Partner talk • Student collaborative reports • Play: Practicing new language structures	*Synthesis* • I learned that . . . • I think that . . . • I noticed that . . . *Sequencing* • First . . . then • The first step is . . .then *Evaluating* • I think this is important because . . . • This is important because . . .	• Layers • Canopy • Emergent • Forest floor • Climate • Location Equator • Evaporation • Condensation • Precipitation • Camouflage

Theory-to-Practice Connection

Jackie's planning charts take into account the need to expand the language of the students at the same time that she incorporates the concepts and the thinking skills that the unit requires. See the introduction to Chapter 4.

BREAKING THE PLAN INTO DOABLE PARTS

Assessing and Developing Background Knowledge

Overview: Getting children to relate to this topic

Jackie started the thematic unit on the rainforest by showing videos, photos, and illustrations in order to give her students a clear idea of what a rainforest is. She felt that visuals would provide a good starting point for her students to interpret the concepts she was going to introduce throughout the unit. Every student had a journal where he or she wrote or drew new facts and new vocabulary.

Visuals and audiovisuals

She introduced the unit by showing a video, *Travel to the Rainforest*, which can be found at http://www.thewildclassroom.com/video/index.html on the Wild Classroom website. This is a video that shows different aspects of the rainforest in Panama: the variety of plant and animal life, the climate, and the layers of the rainforest. It is specially designed for younger viewers as it provides explanations easy to understand. Before showing the video, the teacher planned carefully how she was going to introduce it, and she also developed a video chart that the students would have to fill in during and after the video showing.

Jackie showed short segments focusing on different characteristics of the rainforest. Before she showed the video, she selected the elements that she wanted her students to focus on:

- What is a rainforest?
- Where are the rainforests in the world?
- Layers of the rainforest and animals that live in each layer
- Rainfall in the rainforest
- Destruction of the rainforest

Here are the steps that Jackie followed for every segment she showed her students:

1. **She introduced the video and summarized the portion she was going to show:** "Today, we are going to learn about the layers of the rainforest. Pay attention because you have to take notes in your video chart."

2. **She stated the purpose of the video:** "We are watching this segment of the video in order to understand that enormous amounts of rainfall are one of the characteristics of the rainforest."

3. **She introduced some of the challenging vocabulary** her students were going to encounter before each segment: *layers, moist, diversity, habitats, canopy, understory layer, shrub layer,* and *forest floor*.

4. **She categorized the information** by providing categories for students: *layers*, *climate*, *animal and plant variety*, and *destruction of the rainforest*.

5. **She used selected scenes**, showing each segment several times and holding classroom conversations after the video.

6. **Group work:** She divided the students into small groups to fill in the video chart shown in Table 7.3, focusing on a specific aspect of the video.

Theory-to-Practice Connection

The teacher was careful to provide information that would build her students' background knowledge. This will facilitate the progressive understanding of new concepts. See Chapter 1.

After each video segment, students worked with their partners on completing the part of the chart that related to what they had watched.

Table 7.3 Note-Taking Chart Organizer for *Travel to the Rainforest*

Complete during the video	Complete after the video
————————————————▶	————————————————▶
The things that I have learned about the rainforest	**Write two things you found interesting**
Layers 	
Climate 	

(Continued)

| **Table 7.3** | (Continued) |

Animal and plant variety 	
Where are the rainforests? 	
What is destroying the rainforest?	

Scaffolding the chart organizer for beginning EL students

While the rest of the class worked on their chart organizer, Jackie pulled the EL students who needed more support; showed them portions of the video again; and broke the chart up into several steps, helping them fill in the information. She allowed the very new arrivals to tell her what they understood and wrote the information for them. She wanted everyone to participate in this exercise. Students completed a new chart for each segment (see Table 7.4).

After this group of students completed the first chart, they were asked to work in pairs to fill in the rest of the charts (see Table 7.5). The teacher guided them in this process by reminding them of what they had watched:

Table 7.4 Note-Taking Chart Organizer 1 for EL Students: *Travel to the Rainforest*

The things that I learned about the rainforest	Write two things you found interesting
Layers The tallest layer is called _____ Below the Emergent layer is the _____ layer Below the Canopy layer is the _____ layer Below the Understory is the _____ layer	

Teacher   We learned that different animals live in each layer. For example, ants live in the forest floor. Can you think of other animals that live in the forest floor? Were there any animals in the rainforest that you did not know about? Can you remember in which layer they live?

Through her use of the video and the note-taking charts, Jackie triggered and developed background knowledge to prepare her students for the concepts that she was going to teach in this thematic unit.

Table 7.5   Note-Taking Chart Organizer 2 for EL Students: *Travel to the Rainforest*

Complete during the video	Complete after the video
———————————————▶	———————————————▶
The things that I have learned about the rainforest	Write two things you found interesting
Animal and plant variety Different animals and plants exist in each layer Here are some examples: ————————————— ————————————— —————————————	

Theory-to-Practice Connection

Here the teacher helps the students organize the new information they have received through the video, by providing them with graphic organizers that include visuals, in order to facilitate comprehension. See Chapter 1.

SOCIAL STUDIES AND MATH CONCEPTS

Using Pictures, Visuals, and Picture Books to Understand Concepts of Geography and Climate

Geography

Using a globe, Jackie showed her students where the Equator was, and then she explained that all the rainforests are situated in proximity to the Equator. The teacher said, *"Think about the Equator as an imaginary belt around the world. It is in the middle of the Earth. All the places that are around this belt have warm and rainy weather. These are the perfect ingredients for a rainforest. All rainforests exist within a certain distance to the Equator.*" She asked her students from Brazil, the Dominican Republic, and Haiti to describe the weather in their home countries. The students described how green and big plants were and the torrential rains that fell often; they said the weather was hot and humid. The teacher pointed to a large world map on the wall showing where the students came from and the distance of their countries to the Equator. Because all the students in this class are immigrants, they already had some geographical concepts and had already learned about the continents in previous lessons. Piggybacking on the explanations of her students, she underlined that being geographically close to the Equator means that it will be hot with a lot of rain: a key characteristic of the rainforest. She drew two lines showing how close the rainforests were to the Equator on the wall map.

Every student had an unlabeled world map. The teacher asked them to work with their partners to identify the location of continents, oceans, and the Equator on the large wall map and to color the areas on their maps where the rainforests are located. They had access to other picture books to review the information and to add additional details. For this activity, she paired the new arrivals with more experienced students, so that those students had help in completing the task.

Climate

The teacher then read excerpts from the picture book *Eye Wonder: Rainforest* (Greenwold & Sharman, 2001). One excerpt entitled "Where in the World" described the location of tropical forests around the world with a clear illustration and the weather conditions of places located around the Equator. Then, she read a segment entitled "Weather Forecast," which in very few words described the hot and humid weather of the jungle and stated that rainfall in the rainforest falls at an average of 160 inches a year—some rainforests have as much as 400 inches of rainfall a year.

She reviewed with her students the unit measures of inches and feet, then she asked her students to measure themselves against a tape measure she had posted on the wall. She had prepared a chart showing the proportion of rainfall compared to her height (see Figure 7.6).

Figure 7.6	Comparison of Height With Rainfall Amount

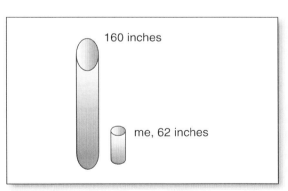

Students spent a few minutes measuring themselves against a measuring chart on the wall and comparing their height with the amount of average rain in the rainforest. They were amazed by how much rain was in 160 inches.

As a follow-up activity, students were asked to find out how much rain falls in New Jersey and compare that to the rainfall in the rainforest. Jackie had posted a chart with the average rainfall in several parts of the United States, so students working in heterogeneous language proficiency groups had to gather the information and compare it with the information they had about the rainforest. After they gathered the information (it rained an average of 50 inches in NJ), the students subtracted the amounts of rain from the rainforest and NJ, and realized that it rained 110 inches more in the rainforest.

The teacher used the opportunity to teach the greater than (>) and less than (<) concepts and symbols. She adapted an idea from "Songs for Teaching" (www.songsforteaching.com/mathsongs.htm) in which children learn to think of the symbol < as an alligator mouth that is always ready to eat the greater number and the symbol > as a closed alligator mouth. She wrote on the board: 110 > 50.

Teacher   The alligator mouth is swallowing the larger number. This means 110 is greater than 50.

The teacher then asked the students to compare the rainfall in other parts of the country with the rain in the rainforest and list the numbers listing them using the symbols > and <.

Finally, Jackie showed the children how to create a graph bar to illustrate the difference of average rainfall between the rainforests and New Jersey. The whole group created the graph bar shown in Figure 7.7.

Figure 7.7 Graph Bar

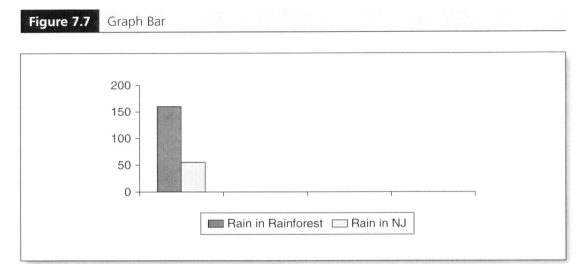

Through these activities, Jackie combined geographical, science, and mathematical concepts to explain rainfall as one of the major characteristics of the rainforest.

SCIENCE

Building a Terrarium to Simulate a Rainforest

Ms. O'Neil planned a science experiment to show her students how the rainforest ecosystem functions, to record how plants grow in that environment, and to learn how the rain cycle works in the rainforest.

The day before the experiment, the teacher read a section about water in the rainforest from the book *A Walk in the Rainforest* (Pratt, 1992). This section describes the enormous amounts of rain that fall in rainforests. After reading the segment, the teacher posed the following question to the class:

When it rains in the rainforest, where do you think the water comes from, and what happens to it after it rains? Turn and tell your partner what you think.

After a lively discussion among the children, the teacher continued:

Teacher   Let's share.

Juan   The water go to the rivers, and it come from the sky.

Adan   Not from the sky, from clouds, and it falls in the ground or in rivers.

Teacher	You are both right. The water comes from the clouds, and it goes both to rivers and to the ground. Tomorrow, we are going to create miniature rainforests inside empty 2-liter soda bottles. These are called terrariums. Then, we will learn how after it rains, something happens that allows water to go back to the clouds. That is called evaporation.

She wrote the words *evaporation, condensation,* and *precipitation* on the board and also wrote their cognates in Spanish for the children who speak Spanish: *evaporación, condensación,* and *precipitación.* Understanding that those words were cognates helped several students to figure out the meaning.

Jackie then asked the class, *"Have you ever watched your mother boil water? What happens if you don't turn off the burner?"*

Julia	The water go away. . . .
Teacher	The water does not go away. It evaporates. It changes from liquid to water vapor.
Julia	Yes, it [the water pot] beeps and the water dries up.
Teacher	It does not dry up. It becomes a mist; that is what we call water vapor.
Teacher	When you wash your hands and don't dry them, what happens to the water in your hands?
Roberto	It get dry by themself.
Teacher	No, the water does not disappear. The water evaporates, it goes up; it turns into tiny droplets—what we call water vapor. And all that water that has evaporated goes up to the clouds, eventually, it condenses as it becomes drops of water; that's what clouds are. The condensed water then falls down on the ground again as rain, or precipitation.
Julia	This what happen in the rainforest?
Teacher	Think about what happens when you boil water; in the rainforest because of the heat from the sun, water turns into tiny droplets (tiny little drops) of water—as we said before, this is water vapor. Then, when they condense, they collect and become larger drops, and they fall back as rain. That is called precipitation.

Theory-to-Practice Connection

Through a whole-class conversation, the teacher helped her students to understand how the water cycle works. She used the understandings the students already had to build on the concepts she wanted to teach. See Chapter 2.

The teacher then showed students a graphic of the water cycle (Figure 7.8).

Then, with student input, she connected the new words with the concepts behind them (Figure 7.9).

Figure 7.8 The Water Cycle

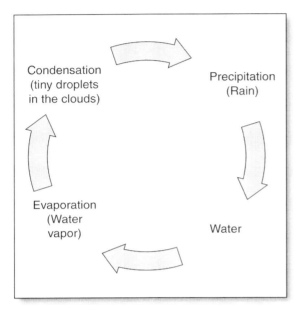

The students wrote the words in their rainforest journals, in the section reserved for vocabulary they were learning through this unit. The teacher added the words to the unit word wall and told students to place a check mark next to the word every time they used it in their conversations or in their writing. They could also put a checkmark if they recognized it in their reading. This worked as a great enticement for the students to use and to look out for these words.

On the day of the experiment, the teacher reminded her students of the meaning of the three words and reviewed the concepts behind them. She then got them ready to work on the terrariums. She started by going over the materials they would need to build their terrariums. Holding up samples of each item they were going to use, she showed the students such things as an empty 2-liter soda bottle, a bag of gravel, and a bag of activated charcoal as she reviewed the vocabulary, explaining to students what each item was.

Figure 7.9 Word Webs

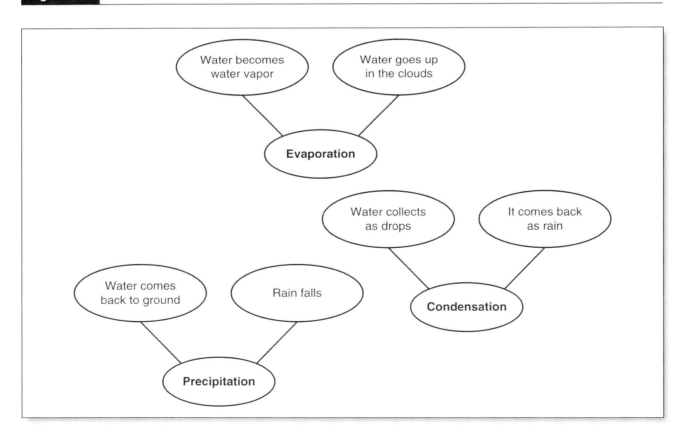

She had a list of the materials with explicit pictures next to each item on chart paper (Figure 7.10).

Figure 7.10 Materials We Need to Build a Terrarium

After reviewing the materials, Jackie wrote the instructions on the board, explaining each step to the students. She invited them to read these words with her in a shared reading exercise. She used the opportunity to use sequencing words, integrating this language goal to the experiment.

How to Build a Terrarium

First, we cut the top of the soda bottle.

After that, we create a mixture that imitates the soil of the rainforest in each bottle: 1 inch of gravel, 1 inch of activated charcoal, and 1 inch of potting soil.

Next, we place the seeds and plants covering the roots with the soil and the moss.

Afterwards, we water the plants lightly.

Then, we tape the top of the soda bottles.

Finally, we cover the top of the bottles with plastic wrap and secure the plastic wrap with rubber bands.

The students worked in pairs to build their terrariums, labeled their bottles with their names, and placed then on top of a shelf by the classroom window where they would get indirect light. They were asked to keep daily notes on the progress of their plants in their journals. For example, they recorded the date when the first lima bean sprouts emerged. They measured the growth of the plants with rulers. For the first few days, they were told that their terrariums may need some extra water, but once the plants began to grow the terrarium would be a self-sustaining environment.

The teacher reminded the students that when the water in the soil evaporates it condenses: It will become moisture and drip on the sides of the bottles watering the plants, and again it will evaporate. This cycle repeats itself over and over again.

Students were asked to:

- Summarize the steps they followed in making their terrariums.
- Measure the plants with a ruler, to note their growth.
- Monitor the level of humidity by observing that water was collecting on the sides of the bottle.

Ms. O'Neil wanted to make sure that her students understood the connection between the experiment and how it relates to the conditions in the rainforest. She supported her students' understanding of how sunlight affects the water cycle by asking them specific and open-ended questions. Here are some of the questions that she posed:

- Since we only watered our terrarium once, why is water collecting on the inside of the bottle?
- What happens to the water that gets collected on the sides of the bottle?
- How do the plants survive without you watering them?

Through this experiment, the students in Ms. O Neil's class were able not only to understand the water cycle but to apply this concept to the conditions that characterize the rainforest.

Theory-to-Practice Connection

Through this experiment, the teacher not only helped the students understand the concept of the "water cycle," but in addition she used the opportunity to teach sequence words, which are parts of the language goals of the unit, in context. See the introduction to Chapter 4.

LANGUAGE ARTS

Read Aloud

Developing nonfiction reading skills through read aloud

Before starting this unit, Jackie collected a large amount of books about the rainforest at different reading levels. She knew that there are very few nonfiction books at a reading level that many of her students could read, but the pictures and the captions could give them some information, and she decided that through read alouds and shared reading activities she could provide the information her students need. Students spent 15 minutes at the beginning of the day looking through the books and sharing their opinions about the pictures and, for those students that could read them, about the text. During read aloud time, the teacher read some nonfiction books, as well as fiction and narrative nonfiction.

The teacher decided to read *Rainforests* (O'Mara, 1996) because it contains basic concepts about the rainforest without too much language overload, and it has very detailed illustrations on each page to show children what the author is describing. Here are the steps she took before she started the book:

1. She asked children to predict what the book is about by looking at the title.

2. She showed the children the table of contents. As she went over it, the children made comments like

   - "this chapter is about the layers of the rainforest" or
   - "this chapter is about the people of the rainforest."

Jackie knew that her students needed help in learning to determine the main idea of each section. She wanted them to focus on the central idea and not on the extra details that each section described. She drew a large chart where she listed the main ideas. The chart had an additional column listing the new vocabulary they were learning through the book. She often stopped to explain new words in context or gave definitions on the run: *"rainfall, that means rain"* or *"layers, remember that means the different levels of the rainforest."*

The new vocabulary words were added to the unit word wall. As she began to read, she drew the children's attention to the title of each section and back to the table of contents, so that children understood that in this book every page had a title that was part of the table of contents. She read the chapter entitled "Tropical Rainforests" in which the author describes the main characteristics of the rainforest—they are located near the Equator, there is an enormous amount of rainfall—and their locations around the world. Then, she showed them a picture of a rainforest and the caption describing it. She explained to them what a caption is.

Jackie started by doing think alouds to figure out the main idea of each section: *"I wonder what the main idea of this section is"* or *"What is this saying?"* As she read through a few chapters, the children discovered that the first sentence of each section gave them the main idea for the section. They then noticed that as the section went on, it gave them more details to support the information of the main idea or extra details. After the third section, children gave Jackie the main idea as she read the chapter. The teacher added what they said to the chart (Table 7.11).

At the end of this activity, Jackie asked her students to look for the main idea when they were reading independently and to list the main idea for each section of their nonfiction books on a sticky note.

Table 7.11 Main Idea Chart

Main Ideas	New Vocabulary
Page 5	
• Tropical rainforests have a heavy rainfall; they are located in the tropics near the Equator, where it is warm and humid • More kinds of plants and animals live in the rainforest than anywhere else on earth	• Tropics • Equator
Page 6	
• Rainforests have four layers: the emergent layer, the canopy, the understory, and the ground layer	• Layers 　1. Emergent layer 　2. Canopy 　3. Understory 　4. Ground layer
Page 7	
• People have lived in the rainforest for thousands of years	• Variety • Humid

Collaborative Projects and Presentation

After reading the book, Jackie wanted her students to apply the information they had gathered and to work collaboratively on a project and a presentation, work that was done over several days. The purpose of this activity was for students to learn about the layers of the forest and to do research on the variety of life specially adapted for that layer:

1. She divided the students into four groups, mixing new-arrival students with more proficient speakers.

2. She assigned each group a layer of the rainforest to do research about the kinds of animals and plants that live in each layer. She had a set of picture books on each table with lots of information. Students took notes on index cards.

3. She asked each group of students to organize the presentation, write what they had discovered, and go in front of the class as a group to present it to their classmates. They were asked to use some of the illustrations from the books they used to show the class examples of the variety of life in their assigned layer.

4. Students were asked to make a drawing depicting the layers of the rainforest with pictures of the animals and plants in that layer.

Figure 7.12 shows two examples of the students' drawing.

Through this activity, students had to apply research skills, take notes, and organize the information in order to present it. This gave them an opportunity to synthesize the information and provided space for them to discuss what they were learning with their partners. Finally, they applied what they had learned by drawing accurate depictions of a layer of the rainforest.

Figure 7.12 Examples of Students' Drawings

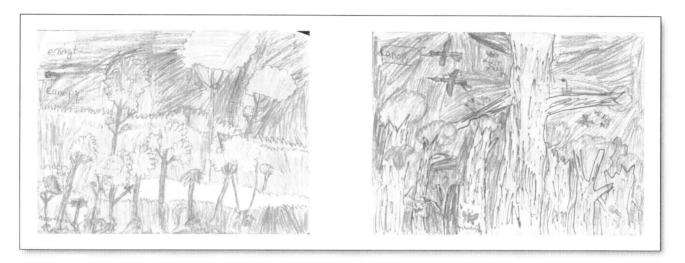

Theory-to-Practice Connection

In this activity the students worked in collaborative groups and had opportunities to discuss their learning with their group partners. In addition, they had to organize their thoughts and elaborate on their ideas during their presentations. These interactions are key elements in order to help students develop academic language. See Chapter 2.

Using narrative nonfiction to further develop concepts and reading skills

To give her students an idea of the interdependency and variety of life that exists in the rainforest, Jackie read *The Great Kapok Tree* by Lynne Cherry (1990). She chose this book because it takes kids to a higher level of understanding of the rainforest: interdependence and deforestation.

Scaffolding the read aloud for ELs and struggling students

Before she started the read aloud to the whole class, the teacher pulled aside her struggling EL students and gave them a picture walk through of the text. She reviewed with them some of the words she thought would be challenging for this group: *Kapok tree*, *humid*, *oxygen*, *wither*, and *chop*. Although she was going to review the same words with the whole class later on, she felt these students needed to hear them more than once. By the time she sat down to do the read aloud with the whole class, her beginning EL students already had a context for what she was going to read.

Creating a bubble graph to review concepts

Before reading the book to the whole class, Jackie decided to use a bubble graphic organizer (which is similar to a KWL chart; see Figure 7.13) to review the information the students had gathered about the rainforest through their previous activities. She asked the children to think about concepts they had learned about the rainforest. As the children described what they had learned, she wrote those words on the inside circle. She reviewed the concepts behind the words so that students who needed to be reminded would, once more, learn what these words meant: *"humid, when it is hot and sticky"* or *"Equator, that imaginary line in the middle of the earth."*

After reading this book, the teacher planned to come back to the circle and add the new concepts the children had learned from the read aloud. Through this activity, she was triggering background knowledge, helping them to synthesize what they had already learned, as well as getting them ready to integrate new information gathered from the read aloud.

Figure 7.13 Bubble Graphic, Part 1

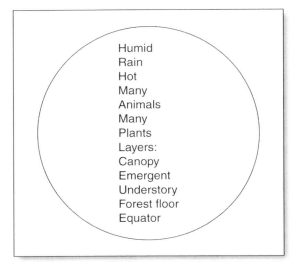

Learning about interdependence

Jackie wanted to work on the concept of interdependence as she read the book. She also wanted to work on one particular reading skill: inferencing. This book provides many opportunities for children to think beyond the text, in understanding how the animals depend on each other and on the tree to survive. Through this read aloud, she could have worked also on skills such as predicting or using strategies to deal with difficult vocabulary, but she felt that her students needed help in this particular skill.

The teacher posted several language prompts around the meeting area and asked students to use them in the discussions about the book and when they spoke with their partners:

I think that . . . because . . .

I agree with . . . because . . .

I disagree with . . . because . . .

The teacher read the book carefully several times before reading it to the class, placing sticky notes at places where she thought her students could gather information and figure out what was important about that particular segment and where they could see how all living things in an ecosystem are interrelated.

She introduced the book by asking students to predict what the book was going to be about just by looking at the title: *The Great Kapok Tree. A Tale of the Amazon Rain Forest* (Cherry, 1990). Her students predicted correctly that the book was about a big tree in the Amazon rainforest; she then gave them a picture walk through of the book, summarizing the story: *"The book tells the story of a man that is sent to the Amazon rainforest to cut a great kapok tree; many animals watch him nervously because they are afraid to lose their habitat, this means their home. A habitat is a home that animals and plants share and depend on to survive. He falls asleep, and animals from the different layers of the forest come down to beg him not to cut the tree because they will not survive without it. When he wakes up, he realizes that there are wonderful animals that depend on that tree and decides not to cut it."*

As Jackie began to read, she stopped at strategic parts of the book and asked her students to retell the segment to their partner and to discuss how cutting the tree would affect the animals:

Julia   I think that the man is going to feel sorry after he wakes up.

Roberto   I disagree with you because he needs the money.

The teacher had a chart hanging on her board divided into two sections: "What the Book Says" and "What This Means" (Table 7.14). Each time students talked to their partners, she wrote some of the ideas on the chart.

Table 7.14 Inference Chart

What the Book Says	What This Means
The man gets tired and falls asleep.	*He stops cutting the tree.*
The boa constrictor says the tree is his home.	*Without the tree, the boa will die.*
Bees have their hives on the tree.	*Without the tree, they could not spread the seeds and flowers and plants will die.*
The monkeys say that the roots of the trees hold onto the soil. Without the roots, the earth will be washed away by rain.	*Rainforests will disappear if the trees are cut. Also, without the trees, monkeys cannot live because they cannot move from place to place.*
The jaguar needs the tree to hunt his food.	*The jaguar will die without food.*
Porcupines say humans and animals need oxygen to live.	*Without plants releasing oxygen, animals and humans will die.*

Throughout the reading, the teacher stopped often, modeling for her children her reactions to the text and her interpretation through think alouds:

> *I'm thinking that there is an idea here that the writer keeps repeating.*
>
> *I think that the animals are trying to give the forest man an idea. What could that be?*

After reading the book, Ms. O'Neil led a whole-class conversation. She posed guiding questions to focus the conversation:

- Why did the author, Lynne Cherry, write this book?
- What is the most important lesson we can learn from this book?

After the students discussed their ideas, she asked, "Can you think of examples of how the animals in the story were dependent on each other and on the kapok tree?" Then, after the children gave examples from the book, she said, "Can you think about ways in which we are dependent on each other in our community?" In this way, she pushed the thinking of the students to relate the concept of interdependence to their own environments.

Theory-to-Practice Connection

Through her think alouds during read aloud, the teacher modeled a reading comprehension strategy, *inference*, and gave her students time to practice making inferences. See Chapter 3.

Finally, Ms. O'Neil brought out the bubble chart she introduced at the beginning of the book, so that her students could add the new information they gathered during the read aloud. She posted the conversation prompts she wanted her students to practice as they were evaluating the new information they gathered from the book:

_____ is important because. . . .

I learned that _____

She drew another circle and wrote down the ideas the children shared (see Figure 7.15).

Figure 7.15 Bubble Graphic, Part 2

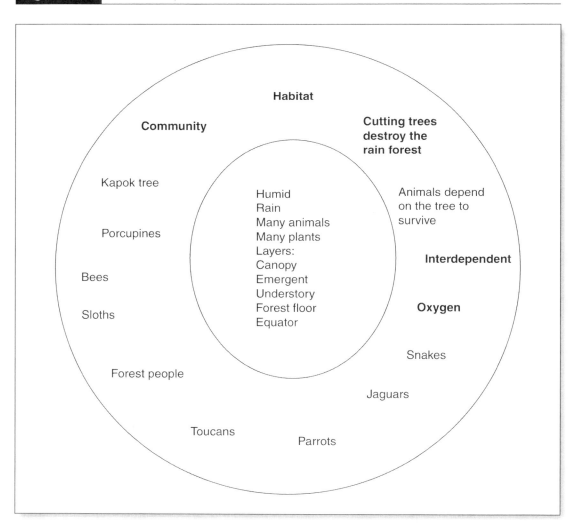

Figure 7.16 Shared Reading

What is camouflage? *home*

Animals need to survive in their environment. They need to hide from their enemies.

pattern

Some animals have special markings or color on their bodies. That allows them to

match *disguise*

blend with their environment. We call this camouflage. It is an animal's way of

hunters

hiding from predators.

The most common form of camouflage is green or brown because these colors are often

found in nature. The frog in this picture is green, it can hide under and behind the leaves.

When the frog is not moving, it is difficult for other

under

animals to see it. Sometimes it sits beneath a plant and

it cannot be discovered.

Some animals have patterns on their body. Leopards, giraffes and jaguars have spots.

hide

The spots help them camouflage. The jaguar in this

picture is standing on a tree branch and he is difficult

to see.

Some reptiles have yellow or brown skin. How can these

colors help them hide? Red and yellow on a snake's skin

deadly

means "I'm poisonous, keep out."

Can you think of ways in which you could blend or camouflage in your environment?

The teacher then reviewed the new information that the children had gathered through their read aloud, making sure that all students understood the concepts behind the words they had listed.

Shared Reading

Working with language structures and vocabulary

Ms. O'Neil decided to introduce the concept of *camouflage*, since this is one of the elements that allows animals to survive in the rainforest. At the same time, she wanted to develop some of the vocabulary associated with this concept.

Gathering the information she had learned from different books, she wrote a shared reading text, adding pictures. She read the text twice with her students using fluency and intonation. Then, she began to work on vocabulary. Only after the text had been read a couple of times did the teacher begin to work on the vocabulary. She chose words that were relevant to the concept of camouflage, and she covered her target words with sticky notes (see Figure 7.16 on page 159). Some words were Tier 3 or technical words, such as *camouflage* or *environment*. These words were covered with sticky notes that presented a Tier 1 equivalent: *hide* for *camouflage* and *home* for *environment*. Other words were covered with equivalent synonyms, such as *match/blend*. Sometimes the students didn't know the equivalent, and she let them discover it:

Teacher   Can we think about another word for environment?

             (No answer)

Teacher   Rodolphe, would you like to come and see what word is under the sticky note?

Rodolphe   (Taking the sticky note off and reading); Home.

Teacher   Let's read it together. Animals need to survive in their home. So environment is like . . .

Students   Home.

By doing this exercise, Jackie integrated vocabulary and content. She was able to teach technical words by associating them with more common words. She accomplished this by using a shared reading text that offered strong contextual support. Even her new arrivals were able to understand the text and participate. As students worked on the new words, she listed them on a chart (Table 7.17) to make it easy for them to see.

Table 7.17 Technical Words

Words We Know	Words We Can Add to Our Vocabulary
Home	Environment
Disguise/Hide	Camouflage
Match	Blend
Looks like	Blends
Under	Beneath
Deadly	Poisonous

The teacher then created a web for each word so that the students could relate the new vocabulary to what they already know (see Figure 7.18).

Theory-to-Practice Connection

In this example, the teacher is using Tier 1 words to teach Tier 2 and 3 words. See Chapter 1.

Working with prepositions using the same shared reading text

Ms. O'Neil noticed that some of her students had trouble with prepositions. Her Spanish-speaking students confused *in* and *on* frequently. Even her more fluent students had trouble in this area. Before working with the shared reading text, she played a game with her students:

Figure 7.18   Word Web

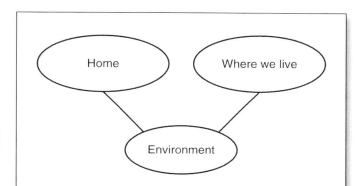

Hide **under** the desk.

Stand **on** your chair.

Put your notebook **in** your bag.

Put your hands **behind** your chair.

Put your shoes **beneath** your chair.

She said, "All those words, *under*, *on*, *in*, *behind*, *beneath*, indicate position. They tell us where things are. We are going to learn how to use them correctly."

For this reading, the teacher covered the prepositions on the shared reading text with blank sticky notes. She had a list of the prepositions on the board: *on*, *in*, *under*, *behind*, and *beneath*. She asked students to figure out the correct preposition in the text with their partners. As children chose the preposition, the teacher uncovered it and they found out if their choice was right.

Animals need to survive **in** their *environment*.

Camouflage is a color or marking **on** an animal's body.

The work on prepositions was extended throughout the unit. Ms. O'Neil wrote other shared reading texts to work on vocabulary, different prepositions, and concepts about the rainforest that she wanted children to understand.

Writing nonfiction texts: Using shared writing to scaffold the process

Since this classroom has such a variety of academic and linguistic levels, Ms. O'Neil decided to allow her students to choose a topic about the rainforest that they would write about for their book reports. She wanted her students to choose a topic that they could teach the rest of the class. Students who had more academic proficiency wrote more detailed reports about the rainforest. Some students chose to write about a particular layer of the rainforest and the animal and plant variety that existed in that layer, while other students chose to write about the dangers facing the rainforests. Some students did research on forest tribes. The students who needed more support were steered towards writing about one particular animal in the rainforest so that their research would be easier, and they were told their reports could be mostly drawings with captions underneath. For Ms. O'Neil, the important thing was that every student be engaged in a research project that was going to end in a book report.

Students were asked to create a structure to organize all the information they had about their particular topic. The teacher modeled the process first by showing them how she would write a book about the rainforest. She said, *"I think I will plan my Table of Contents first, in order to organize my thoughts into chapters. This may change, but at least I will have an idea about how to organize my work."*

During a shared writing activity, she discussed with the students what would go first into the Table of Contents. Children suggested that it start with what the rainforest is. Then, she wondered what would go next. As the students provided ideas, she wrote down the following:

The Rainforest

Table of Contents

1. What is the rainforest?
2. What are the layers of the rainforest?
3. What animals live in the rainforest?
4. Do people live in the rainforest?
5. Why are rainforests important?

She then said to her students, *"This is just an example of a Table of Contents; you may have other ideas about your report."* She asked the students to do research in the classroom as well as in the library. Since these were her more proficient students, she told them she expected them to elaborate on their facts within each section of their report.

Scaffolding this concept for the students who needed more support, Jackie worked with them in the same way, through a shared writing activity, to show them how their Table of Contents might look, using their suggestions as she wrote.

My Book About Jaguars

Table of Contents

1. Where does the jaguar live?
2. The jaguar's body
3. What does the jaguar eat?

She worked closely with this group, helping them select an animal and reading with them interesting facts about the animal of their choice. Some students who were not ready to write a report were encouraged to draw, labeling their drawings with just a few words.

Figure 7.19 shows one page of Jacobo's report on Anacondas.

Figure 7.19   Jacobo's Report on Anacondas

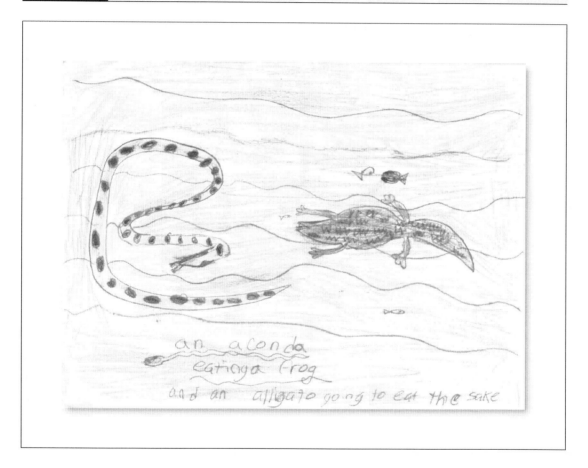

Figures 7.20 and 7.21 show two pages of Riama's report on spiders in the Amazon.

After students wrote a number of pages for their book reports, the teacher asked them to begin to revise what they had written. She asked them to revise their facts or to try to figure out what may confuse their readers. They worked with their partners, reading to each other and responding to their questions. When they finished writing, they presented their reports to the class during several class meetings. Parents were invited to attend. Every student in this class did research and completed the assignment regardless of her or his linguistic or academic ability.

Figure 7.20 Riama's Report on Spiders: Black Widow Body

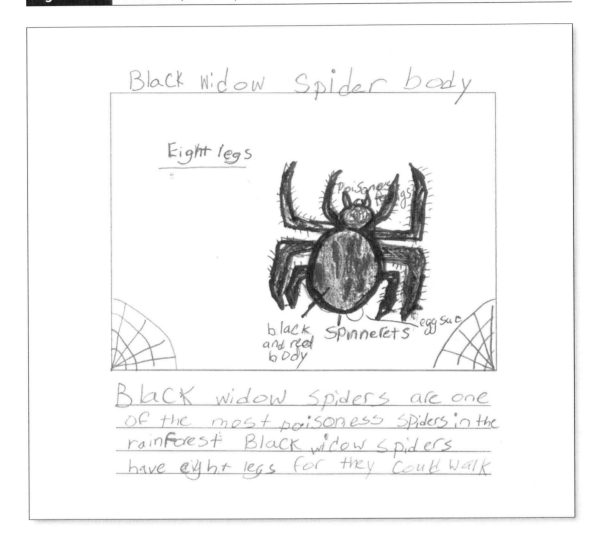

THE RAINFOREST OF THE AMAZON: THE PLAY

Ms. O'Neil felt that a good way to wrap up this unit was to write a play on the Amazon rainforest. The children wanted to write the play based on the story of *The Great Kapok Tree*, which they loved.

The teacher thought this would be a great culminating activity, where the children could show to other children what they had learned, and where they could let their imagination run. She thought there were many benefits in creating a play. Roles could be assigned according to the interest and language skills of each child. Every student would have a part, including the newcomers.

Figure 7.21   Riama's Report on Spiders: Where Black Widow Live

It would provide children with opportunities to

- practice using language, to incorporate and use new words and structures that they had read in the book; and

- reinforce the concepts of interdependence and the importance of rainforests around the world.

The box titled "The Rainforest of the Amazon" shows an excerpt of the script the children created with their teacher's help and a song she wrote for the play. Parents contributed by making the costumes and helping to create the scenery. All students are dressed like animals in the forest.

The Rainforest of the Amazon

By the Second- and Third-Grade Class of Ms. O'Neil

Narrator	The Amazon rainforest is waking up. Deep in the forest we can hear many birds and monkeys. The monkeys make the loudest sounds.

(Children imitate forest and animal sounds in the background.)

(Children walk around the forest, making believe they are eating, jumping, chirping, etc.)

Man	Pedro, go and cut down that big kapok tree. It is a big tree and we can get a lot of wood from it. Hee, hee, hee (He laughs.)
Pedro	I will, I will!!!! (He flexes his muscles and raises the ax.)

(Pedro starts cutting down the tree but he grows tired.)

Pedro	I will take a nap. I am tired. ZZZZZZ (He lays on the floor and snores.)

(As he sleeps, the animals that live in the tree start coming down.)

Boa constrictor and snake	Señor, please don't cut this tree. If you do we will lose our home. We live under this tree. It is dark and humid. It is a perfect home for us.
Monkeys (3 students)	Pedro, please don't cut down this tree. We move around the trees using the vines. We eat its fruits and nuts. If we don't live on a tree, what can we eat? The tree is our home!!!
Bees (3 students)	We all live here, monkeys, toucans, boas. The tree is our home. We find shelter here. If you cut all the trees, all the rainforest will become a desert.
Anteaters (2 students)	And we will have no oxygen.
Two forest people	We have lived in the forest for thousands of years. We respect the forest. Please don't cut the tree.
Pedro (waking up)	I had a sad dream. I have decided not to cut the tree. It is too valuable for the animals that make it their home and also important for humans. If I cut the tree all, the beautiful animals will die, and the forest will die.
Narrator	As the sun falls, all the animals celebrate Pedro's decision. They dance.

(The students sing a forest song to the music of "We Are the Children."

We are the animals,

We are the trees

Our life depends on the trees of the rainforest

Don't cut the trees

Protect the forest

The world will be very poor without us in it.

The students gave two performances to the rest of the school and to the parents. For Ms. O'Neil, this was a culminating activity where her students applied the concepts they had learned and practiced the new language they were learning by enacting the story in front of an audience.

CONCLUSION

Throughout this chapter we have presented a variety of ideas to provide EL students with a curriculum that is rich in content and takes into account their need for expanding their background knowledge as well as learning technical vocabulary associated with the unit. The teacher scaffolded the activities to make sure all students were engaged in the activities, regardless of their linguistic or academic proficiency.

Through the exploration of a broad theme of *the rainforest*, we integrated concepts from different curricular areas: social studies, science, math, and art. In addition, since children had to use expository and informational text to gather information about the rainforest, we used the study of the theme to teach children nonfiction reading and writing strategies, such as getting the main idea, inferencing, and understanding the author's purpose. In this process, the teacher focused on higher order thinking skills.

The development of the unit was supported by many ongoing small-group and whole-class projects where students were able to use the language and concepts that they were learning in a variety of ways: Students had a chance to read, write, and speak independently, with partners, and in whole-group discussions. Above all, even though Ms. O'Neil was working with students who were at different levels academically and linguistically, she held high expectations for all.

Effective thematic planning requires organization, selection of a variety of materials, and knowledge of how to build conceptual and language skills across the different content areas. The effort involved is worth it, since it demonstrates that mastering a topic requires interdisciplinary input.

TEACHER SELF-ASSESSMENT FOR THE UNIT

Have I . . .	
Selected a broad topic that can have multiple points of entry (social studies, language arts, math, science, art)?	
Incorporated learning goals for each curriculum area?	
Incorporated nonfiction reading and writing strategies?	
Included visuals and audiovisuals to reinforce the understanding of different concepts?	

Used shared reading to teach language structures and reinforce concepts?	
Integrated language goals at every step of the unit?	
Made sure students understand the challenging vocabulary and are able to use it?	
Created enough opportunities for children to work collaboratively and have time to discuss and share ideas?	
Scaffolded the work to make sure all students participate?	
Provided opportunities for independent research?	
Provided opportunities for outside retelling?	

Conclusion

Throughout this book, we have tried to demonstrate that when working with English learners and struggling students, teachers can maintain high standards and teach content without watering down the curriculum. We have based our book in our deep belief that learning is inherently a social act, where ideas are clarified and enriched by conversations and interactions. These conversations are the key element to develop academic language; they revolve around an intellectually rich and challenging curriculum. Working with students who have low literacy skills or who are English learners doesn't require a different curriculum; it requires careful and intentional planning.

We have tried to focus on both aspects of learning language: language acquisition and language learning (Krashen, 1997). Across the units in this book, teachers have integrated into their plans opportunities for their students to learn English naturally (language acquisition), through meaningful interactions in the classrooms, and through balanced literacy activities that promote language development. At the same time, there have been specific plans for language learning; we have helped teachers understand how to teach grammatical structures as well as vocabulary, in context, through explicit instruction.

Throughout the four units that were developed, we focused on three key areas to properly scaffold the content:

Developing background knowledge specific to the unit. In each of the units we presented, the point of departure for developing content and language goals was the students' own background knowledge. All teachers we described spent time triggering and developing background knowledge about the topic they were teaching. In addition, they used a variety of teaching tools to present the new content to their students. Through the use of videos, pictures, charts, read alouds, shared reading, shared writing, and graphic organizers, difficult concepts were made accessible to the students without diluting the content, and they, in turn, were required to practice and reflect on what they were learning. The information and concepts that the students received in the course of each unit were reinforced by conversations, class trips, inquiry reports, and class presentations.

Planning for content and language. For every unit we connected the content and language goals. We created the space and the time to focus on content, vocabulary, and language structures. This allowed students to learn language and gain a deeper understanding of the topic. We used a "recycling approach" to language and content instruction using key structures from Balanced Literacy: read aloud, shared reading, and shared writing; concepts that were presented auditorily in read aloud were then targeted in shared reading, allowing students to read and discuss the concepts that they had listened to. Interactions between teachers and students allowed them to move into more sophisticated forms of language in shared writing or outside retellings. This recycling approach allowed students to transfer and gain more understanding by successive interactions with texts and through conversations.

Thinking skills attached to specific language structures and prompts. Each unit contained an array of strategies and scaffolds that supported the development of critical thinking skills. Using Bloom's (1956) taxonomy as a guide, we provided the kinds of questions that could guide the work of the students, as well as the classroom conversations, into higher order thinking skills such as analysis, synthesis, and evaluation. In addition, through language prompts we furnished the language that students could use to apply those skills.

We hope that throughout this book one of our main ideas comes across: Academic language has to be planned; it cannot be left to chance and is not merely a question of exposure. Learning academic language requires opportunities to hear it, to analyze it, and to practice it.

References

Allington R. (2001). *What really matters for struggling readers: Designing research-based programs.* London: Longman.

Altenberg, E. P., & Vago, R. M. (2010). *English grammar. Understanding the basics.* Cambridge, UK: Cambridge University Press.

Argueta, J. (2006). *La Fiesta De Las Tortillas.* Miami, FL: Alfaguara.

August, D., Carlo, M., Dressler, C., & Snow, C. E. (2005). The critical role of vocabulary development for English language learners. *Learning Disabilities Research and Practice, 20*(1), 150–157.

August, D., & Shanahan, T. (2008). *Developing reading and writing in second language learners: Lesson from the Report of the National Literacy Panel on Language Minority Children and Youth.* New York, NY: Routledge.

Baker, C. (2006). *Foundations of bilingual education and bilingualism* (4th ed.). Clevedon, UK: Multilingual Matters.

Beck, I. L., McKeown, M. G., & Kucan, L. (2005). *Bringing words to life.* New York, NY: Guilford.

Beers, K. (2003). *When kids can't read, what teachers can do: A guide for teachers, 6–12.* Portsmouth, NH: Heinemann.

Blachowicz, C. L. Z., & Cobb, C. (2007). *Teaching vocabulary across the content areas.* Alexandria, VA: Association for Supervision and Curriculum Development.

Bloom, B. (1956). *Taxonomy of educational objectives. The classification of educational goals.* New York, NY: Susan Fauer Company.

Bomer, K. (2005). *Writing a life: Teaching memoir to sharpen insight, shape meaning—and triumph over tests.* Portsmouth, NH: Heinemann.

Buehl, D. (2009). *Classroom strategies for interactive learning.* Newark, DE: International Reading Association.

Calkins, L. M. (1994). *The art of teaching writing.* Portsmouth, NH: Heinemann.

Calkins, L. M. (2001). *The art of teaching reading.* New York, NY: Longman.

Cazden, C. B. (1992). *Whole language plus: Essays on literacy in the United States and New Zealand.* New York, NY: Teachers College Press.

Chall, J. S. (1983). *Stages of reading development.* Boston, MA: McGraw-Hill.

Chamot, A. U. (2009). *The CALLA handbook. Implementing the cognitive academic language learning approach* (2nd ed.). Boston, MA: Pearson.

Chen, L., & Mora-Flores, E. (2006). *Balanced literacy for English learners. K–2.* Portsmouth, NH: Heinemann.

Cherry, L. (1990). *The great kapok tree: A tale of the Amazon rain forest.* New York, NY: Harcourt Brace.

Church, S., Baskwill, J., & Swain, M. (2007). *Yes but . . . if they like it they'll learn it. How to plan, organize, and assess learning experiences with meaning, purpose and joy.* Markham, Canada: Pembroke Publishers.

Cisneros, S. (1991). *The house on Mango Street.* New York, NY: Vintage.

Collier, V. (1995). *Promoting academic success for ESL students. Understanding second language acquisition for school.* Jersey City, NJ: Teachers of English to Speakers of Other Languages.

Collier, V., & Thomas, W. (1999). Developmental bilingual education. In F. Genesee (Ed.), *Program alternatives for linguistically and diverse students' long term academic achievement.* Santa Cruz, CA: Center for Research on Education, Diversity and Excellence.

Coxhead, A. (2000). *The academic word list*. Retrieved May 8, 2011, from www.uefap.com/vocab/select/awl.htm

Crews, D. (1992). *Shortcut*. New York, NY: Greenwillow.

Cullinan, B. E. (1993). *Children's voices: Talk in the classroom*. Newark, DE: International Reading Association.

Cummins, J. (1979). Cognitive/academic language proficiency, linguistic interdependence, the optimum age and some other matters. *Working Papers on Bilingualism, 19,* 121–129.

Cummins, J. (1985). The construct of language proficiency in bilingual children. In J. E. Alatis & J. Staczek (Eds.), *Perspectives on bilingualism and bilingual education* (pp. 209–231). Washington, DC: Georgetown University Press.

Cummins, J. (2000). BICS and CALP: Clarifying the distinction. *ED:* 438–551.

Cummins, J. (2007). *Language, power, and pedagogy: Bilingual children in the crossfire*. Clevedon, UK: Multilingual Matters.

Cummins, J., Baker, C., & Hornberger, N. H. (2001). *An introductory reader to the writings of Jim Cummins*. Clevedon, UK: Multilingual Matters.

Cunningham, P. M., & Allington, R. L. (2007). *Classrooms that work: They can all read and write*. Boston, MA: Pearson/Allyn & Bacon.

Delpit, L. D. (2006). *Other people's children: Cultural conflict in the classroom*. New York, NY: New Press.

Dobb, F. (2004). *Essential elements of effective science instruction for English learners*. Los Angeles: California Science Project.

Dong, Y. R. (2004). *Teaching language and content to linguistically and culturally diverse students: Principles, ideas, and materials*. Greenwich, CT: Information Age.

Echevarria, J., Vogt, M., & Short, D. (2000). *Making content comprehensible for English language learners: The SIOP model*. Boston, MA: Allyn & Bacon.

Ellis, R., & Fotos, S. (1999). *Learning a second language through interaction*. Amsterdam: J. Benjamins.

Fillmore, L. W., & Snow, C. E. (2000). *What teachers should know about language, 2000*. Retrieved from http://citeseerx.ist.psu.edu/viewdoc/download?doi=10.1.1.92.9117&rep=rep1&type=pdf

Freeman, D. E., & Freeman, Y. S. (2000). *Teaching reading in multilingual classrooms*. Portsmouth, NH: Heinemann.

Freeman, Y. S., & Freeman, D. E. (2009). *Academic language for English language learners and struggling readers: How to help students succeed across content areas*. Portsmouth, NH: Heinemann.

Gibbons, G. (1994). *Nature's green umbrella: Tropical rain forests*. New York, NY: Morrow Junior.

Gibbons, P. (1991). *Learning to learn in a second language*. Portsmouth, NH: Heinemann.

Gibbons, P. (2006). *Bridging discourses in the ESL classroom*. London: Continuum.

Graves, M. (2005). *The vocabulary book: Learning and instruction* (Language and Literacy Series). New York, NY: Teachers College Press.

Greenfield, E., Jones, L. L., Jones, P. R., & Pinkney, J. (1979). *Childtimes: A three-generation memoir*. New York, NY: Crowell.

Greenwold, E., & Sharman, H. (2001). *Eye wonder: Rainforest*. New York, NY: DK Publishing.

Hall, J., & Walsh, M. (2002). Teacher student interaction and language learning. *Annual Review of Applied Linguistics, 22,* 186–203.

Hart, B., & Risley, T. (2003). *Meaningful differences in the everyday experience of young American children*. Baltimore, MD: Paul H. Brookes.

Harvey, S. (1998). *Nonfiction matters. Reading, writing and research in Grades 3–8*. Portsmouth, NH: Stenhouse Publishers.

Havill, J., & O'Brien, A. S. (1986). *Jamaica's find*. Boston, MA: Houghton Mifflin.

Haynes, J., & Zacarian, D. (2010). *Teaching English language learners across the content areas*. Alexandria, VA: ASCD.

Herbert, J. (2002). *The American Revolution for kids: A history with 21 activities*. Chicago, IL: Chicago Review.

Hudelson, S. (1994). Literacy development of second language children. In F. Genesee (Ed.), *Educating second language children, the whole child, the whole curriculum.* Cambridge, UK: Cambridge University Press.

January, B. (2000). *Colonial life.* New York, NY: Children's Press.

Keene, E. O., & Zimmermann, S. (2007). *Mosaic of thought: The power of comprehension strategy instruction.* Portsmouth, NH: Heinemann.

Krashen, S. D. (1997). *Foreign language education the easy way.* Culver City, CA: Language Education Associates.

Lee, J. F., & VanPatten, B. (2003). *Making communicative language teaching happen.* Boston, MA: McGraw-Hill.

Levy, E. (1987). *If you were there when they signed the Constitution.* New York, NY: Scholastic.

Lipson, M., Valencia, S., Wixson, S. K., & Peters, C. (1993). Integration and thematic teaching: Integration to improve teaching and learning. *Language Arts, 70*(4), 252–263.

Long, M. H. (2007). *Problems in SLA.* Mahwah, NJ: Lawrence Erlbaum.

Malnor, B., & Malnor, C. (1998). *A teacher's guide to a walk in the rainforest.* Nevada City, CA: Dawn Publications.

Marzano, R. J. (2004). *Building background knowledge for academic achievement: Research on what works in schools.* Alexandria, VA: Association for Supervision and Curriculum Development.

Michaels, S., O'Connor, M. C., & Resnick, L. (2007). Deliberative discourse: Idealized and realized: Accountable talk in the classroom and in the civic life. *Studies in the Philosophy in Education, 27*(4), 283–297.

Nagy, W. (1988). *Teaching vocabulary to improve reading comprehension.* Newark, DE: International Reading Association.

Ogle, D. (1986). KWL: A teaching model that develops active reading of expository text. *Reading Teacher, 39,* 564–570.

O'Mara, A. (1996). *Rainforests.* Mankato, MN: Capstone Press: Bridgestone.

Pauk, W., & Ross, Q. W. O. (2007). *How to study in college* (9th ed.). Belmont, CA: Wadsworth.

Paulsen, G., & Paulsen, R. W. (1995). *The tortilla factory.* San Diego, CA: Harcourt Brace.

Pinnell, G. S., & Fountas, I. (2007). *The content of literacy learning 3–8. A guide to teaching.* Portsmouth, NH: Heinemann.

Polacco, P. (1998). *Thank you Mr. Falker.* New York, NY: Philomel.

Pratt, K. J. (1992). *A walk in the forest.* Nevada City, CA: Dawn Publications.

Reiss, J. (2008). *102 content strategies for English language learners. Teaching for academic success in Grades 3–12.* Boston, MA: Pearson/Allyn & Bacon.

Resnick, B. L. (1999). *Making America smarter.* Education Week Century Series. Retrieved from wilsonsd.org

Rylant, C., & Gammell, S. (1985). *The relatives came.* New York, NY: Bradbury.

Sesso, G., & Weller, C. (2000). *The New York State story.* Austin, TX: Steck-Vaughn.

Short, D. (1996). *Integrating language and culture in the social studies: Final report to the U.S. Department of Education, Office of Educational Research and Improvement.* Santa Cruz, CA: National Center for Research on Cultural Diversity and Second Language Learning, U.S. Department of Education, Educational Resources Information Center.

Skutnabb-Kangas, T., & Toukomaa, P. (1976). *Teaching migrant children mother tongue and learning the language of the host country in the context of the sociocultural situation of the migrant family.* Tampere, Finland: Tukimuksia Research Report.

Snow, C. E., Griffin, P., & Burns, S. (2005). *Knowledge to support the teaching of reading. Preparing teachers for a changing world.* San Francisco, CA: Jossey-Bass.

Snow C. E., Porche, M. V., & Tabors, P. O. (2007). *Is literacy enough?* Baltimore, MD: Brookes Publishing Company.

Szpara, M. Y., & Ahmad, I. (2006). *Making social studies meaningful for ELL students. Content and pedagogy in mainstream classrooms.* Retrieved from http://www.usca.edu/essays/v01162006/ahmad.pdf

Vygotsky, L. S., & Cole, M. (1978). *Mind in society: The development of higher psychological processes.* Cambridge, MA: Harvard University Press.

Wexo, J. B. (1999). *Camels.* Evanston, IL: Zoobooks.

Williams, V. B. (1982). *A chair for my mother.* New York, NY: Greenwillow.

Wolf, M. K., Crosson, A. C., & Resnick, L. B. (2006). *Accountable talk in reading comprehension instruction* (CSE Technical Report 670). Pittsburgh, PA: Learning and Research Development Center, University of Pittsburgh.

Yolen, J., & Schoenherr, J. (2007). *Owl moon.* New York, NY: Philomel.

WEBSITES CITED

www.brainpop.com

www.teacherdomain.com

www.nationalgeographic.com

www.birminghamzoo.com/

Southwest Center for Education and the Natural Environment (SCENE): http://scene.asu.edu

VIDEOS

PBS. (2004). *Colonial House.* Alexandria, VA: PBS Home Video.

Videos From the Wild Classroom

http://www.thewildclassroom.com/biomes/rainforest.html

http://www.worldwildlife.org/what/wherewework/amazon/index.html

ENCHANTED LEARNING

http://www.enchantedlearning.com/subjects/rainforest/animals/Rfbiomeanimals.shtml

http://teachersnetwork.org/IMSL/ps6/rainforest.htm

Songs for Teaching® Using Music to Promote Learning: www.songsforteaching.com/mathsongs.htm

ADDITIONAL RESOURCES ON RAINFORESTS

Castaldo, N. F. (2003). *Rainforests: An activity guide for ages 6–9.* Chicago, IL: Chicago Review.

Crandell, R. (2009). *Hands of the rainforest: The Emberá people of Panama.* New York, NY: Henry Holt.

Green, J. (2004). *Rainforest.* New York, NY: DK Revealed Publishing.

Kalman, B., & Crossingham, J. (2001). *What are camouflage and mimicry?* New York, NY: Crabtree.

Mitchell, S. K. (2007). *The rain forest grew all around them.* New York, NY: Sylvan Dell.

Ricciuti, E. R. (1995). *Biomes of the world. The rainforest.* New York, NY: Marshall Cavendish.

Index

The Corwin logo—a raven striding across an open book—represents the union of courage and learning. Corwin is committed to improving education for all learners by publishing books and other professional development resources for those serving the field of PreK–12 education. By providing practical, hands-on materials, Corwin continues to carry out the promise of its motto: **"Helping Educators Do Their Work Better."**

Made in United States
North Haven, CT
14 September 2023

41564087R00111